IN MARTHA'S WAKE

VACATION CRUISING THE CHESAPEAKE BAY

BY
ROBERT E. CLARKE

PHOTOGRAPHY BY
CHRISTER BROMAN
and
CELIA CLARKE

AFFECTIONATELY DEDICATED TO OUR
GRANDAUGHTERS

SOLVEIG AND OLIVIA

IN FERVENT HOPE
THAT THE CHESAPEAKE BAY THEY INHERIT
FINDS THE NECESSARY STEWARDSHIP AND CARE
TO SUSTAIN ITS REMARKABLE BEAUTY.

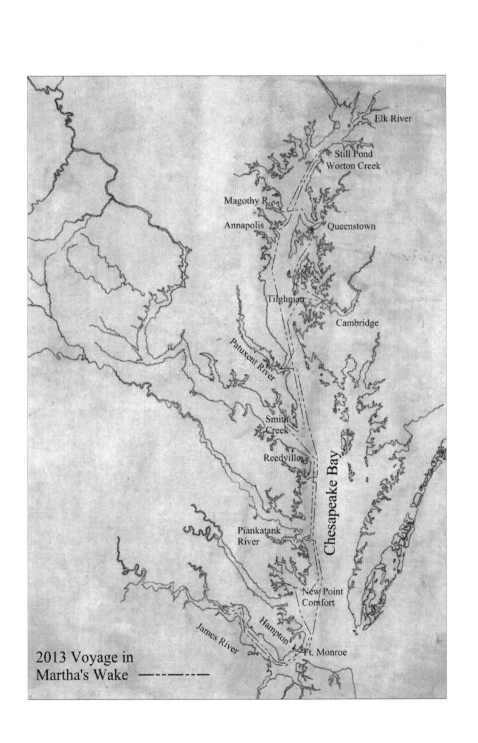

Elk River

Still Pond
Worton Creek

Magothy R.

Annapolis

Queenstown

Tilghman

Cambridge

Patuxent River

Smith
Creek

Reedville

Chesapeake Bay

Piankatank
River

New Point
Comfort

Hampton

James River

Ft. Monroe

2013 Voyage in
Martha's Wake ———————

CONTENTS

"In spite of its storms and its calms, its over-dreaded mosquitoes, and its alleged malaria, I have come to think of the Chesapeake Bay as my sanitarium. I know that I come back from my trips there stronger than when I start on them. It is a soul-expanding process simply to gaze out on the water, to study the features of the headlands, and to conjecture by what time and by what agencies they were formed."

J.T. Rothrock, M.D.

CHAPTER I
DESCRIPTION OF THE YACHT
AND REASON FOR THE CRUISE

I first ran across Joseph Rothrock's *"Vacation Cruising in Chesapeake and Delaware Bays"* while I was researching historic buildings and structures erected along the Chesapeake's shoreline. No body of water in the United States has played a more important role in shaping this nation than has the Chesapeake, and the residual structures and buildings built along its shore stand as a testament to the founding and development of a nation and its people. America was born and came of age along the Bay's waterway, and the fabric of its history still remains recorded in the plantation homes, forts, churches, commercial buildings, boats, historic neighborhoods, lighthouses, and other structures dotting its waterways. Rothrock's book provides a vivid picture of what the Bay once was, and communicates as plainly as an old family portrait what 130 years ago was the condition of the region.

Rothrock's book exists as the first "cruiser's guide" ever written for Chesapeake recreational boating. Long out of print and written in a journal style, the book detailed Rothrock's summer cruise on the thirty foot sloop *Martha* in 1883. For three months Rothrock sailed on both the Chesapeake Bay and the Delaware River in order to "preach" a gospel of relaxation. His book chronicled his journey and spoke of the people, environment, and values of the tidewater. He laid open a detailed analysis of a region that has evolved into something very different. Having sailed the Chesapeake for over 40 years, I was mesmerized by his story, and resolved to one day sail in *Martha's* wake. The year 2013 stands as the 130th anniversary of his voyage, so the time seemed right to follow his journey in a similar search for relaxation and spiritual renewal.

Joseph Trimble Rothrock was born on April 9, 1839, in McVeytown, Pennsylvania, to a German farming family. Educated at Tuscarora Academy of Academia in Juniata County, followed by Freeland Seminary (now Ursinus College) in Montgomery County, Pennsylvania, he went on to attend Harvard College where he graduated with a B.S. in Botany in 1862. During the Civil War, Rothrock enlisted in the Union Army as a private. He eventually rose in the ranks to become a captain in the 20th Pennsylvania Cavalry. During the Battle of Fredericksburg, Rothrock sustained serious injuries that ended his military service. He went on to attend the University of Pennsylvania where he received an M.D. in 1867.

Rothrock's career included work as an educator, a medical practitioner, a botanist, and an environmental scientist. He taught botany, human anatomy, and physiology at the Agricultural College of Pennsylvania (now The Pennsylvania State University) from 1867 to 1869. In 1869, after marrying Martha E. May, Rothrock moved to Wilkes-Barre, Pennsylvania, to practice medicine and to found the Wilkes-Barre Hospital. In 1873, he left his medical practice to concentrate on botanical research. He worked until 1875 as a botanist for the United States Engineers. He went on to take a position at the University of Pennsylvania in Philadelphia as a professor of botany and as a faculty member for the Department of Medicine. In 1877, he was named the Michaux Lecturer for the promotion of botany and forestry, holding this position until 1891.

Rothrock took his summer voyage at forty-four years of age, during his University of Pennsylvania tenure. Of his motivations for taking the journey he writes, *"The plan of spending this vacation on the water grew gradually, and at last commended itself to my judgment, because it was cheap, full of health, and promised as complete a change in mode of life as one could hope to obtain.*

Furthermore, as I proposed partly utilizing the time by such natural history studies and observations as would not consume brain-power faster than it was created, some few books, a microscope, plant-press, and paper were required.

These conditions were most fully met by making a small yacht my means of conveyance, my home, and my laboratory. It is to be remembered that study was far from being the primary object of the cruise."

To place his cruise in historic context, the United States had celebrated its hundredth birthday seven years before the cruise and had conducted a great "Centennial Exposition" in Philadelphia, where new consumer products were displayed, including the telephone, the typewriter, and the Wallace-Farmer Electric Dynamo, precursor to the electric light. Joshua Slocum was twelve years from weighing anchor on his famous cruise around the world when Rothrock weighed anchor himself. Chester A. Arthur had gained the American Presidency twenty-one months before the voyage, after the assassination of President James Garfield in Washington, DC. The United States was still recovering from the political and emotional traumas of the Civil War, and the industrial revolution, with all its progress, was the seminal factor shaping the nation. The country was growing rapidly as waves of new immigrants arrived daily from Europe. And the Brooklyn Bridge was completed and opened just one month before Rothrock set sail.

"To carry out my plan a strong, nearly new boat was purchased, not a racing yacht, in which everything was sacrificed to speed, but a solid, "well-fastened" little sloop, whose qualities were safety first, comfort second, and some speed at the tail-end of a long list of good points.

This boat, originally the "Varuna," of Bridgeton (New Jersey), was renamed "Martha", for reasons which were entirely satisfactory to my little boys (who were my sailing companions part of the time) and to myself. The custom-house papers gave thirty feet long, eleven feet beam, and three and a half feet deep as the dimensions of the little craft."

CamiCat Under Sail

The boats we sailed in *Martha's* wake were of an unknown design to Rothrock. Our Island Packet Cats are production catamarans built for coastal and off shore cruising . They have an overall length of thirty five feet, a length at the water line of thirty one feet, a beam of fifteen feet, displacement of eleven thousand pounds, and draft of only two and a half feet. Our boats were designed by Robert Johnson as cruising catamarans, and unlike Rothrock's, had auxiliary power provided by twin Yanmar diesel engines. Like Rothrock's, our boats were not built as racing yachts but as solid well-fastened sloops designed for safety and comfort.

My sailing companions included the Broman family, sailing an identical Packet Cat. Our *Second Wind*, was commanded by my wife Cece, skippered by me, and crewed by family and friends who joined us for various legs of our journey. The Broman boat, *CamiCat*, was likewise commanded by Camilla and skippered by Christer, who also served as official photographer of the expedition.

"No more sail was carried than was absolutely required. The spars were shorter and stronger than were usual in sloops of her size; and, as further security against a capsize, more than a ton of pig iron was placed and fastened as low down inside as we could get it. Six hundred to a thousand pounds more outside on her keel would have added to her sailing qualities, though without this the boat gave no indication of unsteadiness.

Before the vacation began every seam had been most carefully gone over and made tight; the standing rigging was newly set up, and every cord of the running rigging was either new, or as good as new. Our ground tackle was two powerful holding anchors and plenty of manila rope to swing to. Cleats and reefing gear were all in perfect order. Not once during the entire summer were we endangered or incommoded from want of preparation of anything we should have had ready, but which was not ready.

A good aneroid barometer held a place so conspicuous that it must be noticed, and thus we were left without excuse if not forewarned of coming danger by storm. Compass, charts, lead and line, side-lights, anchor-light, and cabin-light completed the details that contemplated safety.

Next came comfort. First of all, every avenue to the cabin was guarded by wire mosquito-netting, so well guarded that we absolutely escaped all torment from these minute flying fiends. We always kept the sliding cabin windows open. Hence we had the full benefit by day and by night of whatever "air was going." The "bunks" were large enough for men of moderate dimensions to sleep comfortably in, with tossing room besides. The rule that all bedding must be frequently aired was religiously adhered to."

Second Wind's and *CamiCat's* interior layout includes two hulls, each with forward cabins with queen-size bunks and aft head compartments with shower stalls. Between the hulls is the main salon and galley. The main salon is spacious with a dining table and large settee. The decks are wide and the cockpit roomy, with dodger, bimini and cockpit enclosures. The head sail and main sail are both rigged with roller furling, making sail handling an easy chore that can be accomplished from the cockpit. The twin Yanmar diesels with three blade propellers make for easy maneuverability in tight quarters.

Second Wind Enjoying Her Element

Our boats have been outfitted, like the *Martha*, first and foremost for the safety and security of the crew. Equipped to U.S. Coast Guard standards, we carry equipment totally foreign to Rothrock and his times. Life jackets, flares, Life Sling, inflatable life raft and inflatable PFDs are carried for basic crew safety. VHF radios are carried, allowing us to maintain both ship and shore communication. The latest weather predictions are available from VHF and satellite radio, and over cell phones and smart phones which provide accurate real time radar maps. GPS navigation has become the primary method of navigating, with tools to plot and locate our boats to within a single boat-length of accuracy. Emergency medical help is available and accessible by helicopter within minutes. Our safety at sea is light years ahead of Rothrock's, thanks to both technology and the work of the U.S. Coast Guard.

The next priority for the trip was comfort. The boats are outfitted with electric refrigeration, propane stoves, microwave ovens, air conditioning (which proved to be problematic), electric fans, satellite radio, television, and electric LED lights. Each of these comforts was invented and commercially marketed in the past century, and all provide a luxury that would have been unimaginable to Rothrock and his companions on the *Martha*.

"Food - Canned corn, tomatoes, and baked beans, with rice, oatmeal, prunes, good pilot-bread, ham and the best breakfast bacon, tea, coffee, and sugar, I purchased for the season at wholesale price. Fresh fruits and meats were obtained as required. If there was lack of luxurious living, there was no want of nutritious plain food. The medicine-case was well supplied, not that it was needed much for the inmates of the boat, but because, in the out-of-the-way places where we went, it often enabled me to relieve some suffering fellow. There is a comfort in giving help without hope of reward, or without possibility of it, save such mental approval as a pure charity brings to the giver. A little of this does go a long, long way into after-life, softening one's own sorrows, and brightening his own joys. Hence, then, by all means, a medicine-chest."

We provisioned the trip with heavy reliance on our boats' refrigeration systems, and shipped out with frozen meats, fish and vegetables. We refrigerated milk, eggs, cheeses, lunch meats, butter, yogurt and condiments. Cereals, pasta, breads, crackers, canned vegetables, soups, tea, beer, wine and coffee were all stowed in quantity sufficient to meet the needs of a three week cruise. We also shipped with fresh fruits and vegetables that we planned to re-provision in Hampton, VA, and Solomon Island, MD, where groceries would be available within easy reach of our anchorages. Finally, we planned to enjoy the benefits of good restaurants in many of the marinas and towns that we would be visiting.

"Another most important article was added a small, cheap camera for dry-plate photography. One may now be had at a price which is within reach of

every tourist, and nothing is easier than to become an adept in the use of the instrument. Let me suggest, however, that each tourist contemplating a prolonged trip purchase enough plates at once for his use, and that he fairly test their sensitiveness before leaving his base of supplies. I have no complaints to make because a large proportion of the plates of a well known dealer failed to give the results I had anticipated, and which I had always obtained before from his supplies. The fault was my own, that I had not tried the lot before starting out. We can hardly as yet guess how important a factor this amateur photography is to be in the book-making of the future. Neither can we measure its possible influence in opening minds to the quiet beauty or the sublime grandeur which our land everywhere possesses. To judge what its possible effect may be a century hence, study what it has already done for men and women too who, before they became amateurs, had no appreciation of the fact that a tree or a rock could have either individuality or attractiveness. Without wishing to be over-enthusiastic, or be regarded as filled with the zeal of a neophyte, I can hardly avoid counting this art in as one of the humanizing forces of the times."

Christer Retrieving His Plane After Flight

We carried digital cameras for our cruise, and they included small pocket cameras, SLR digital cameras with various lenses, and of most interest, a small model airplane equipped with a GoPro camera allowing us to take aerial pictures of anchorages and sites. Christer, being an accomplished model airplane builder and flyer, fabricates small planes that can be easily launched and recovered from the water or on a short field. The GoPro camera was also modified to "be run up the mast" with camera shots activated by a Bluetooth remote. Downloading photos onto laptop computers allowed us to immediately review and edit the cruise's photography, and unlike Rothrock, left us no surprises in the end.

"Reading matter - What so good as some of Kingsley's writings? Real enough to charm and invigorate the mind, suggestive enough to open whole realms to any student who has the capacity for observation or for generalization, yet without the details with which some authors drag their readers down to the level of those everlasting figures. There is a mental condition which grows out of constantly contemplating ratio and percentage which is dangerous, because the victim always fails to note that the sunshine is leaving his soul, and that, as his facts and his averages pile themselves higher and higher, his own inner self is being dwarfed. Who of all writers could so fitly fill the little space left for reading matter as Charles Kingsley? Of course there were, besides, the ordinary scientific and yachting manuals."

We have again turned to electronics to address our reading needs, and carry Kindles with an ability to download reading material wirelessly whenever in port. In hard copy I carried Rothrock's 1884 book, a copy of *"Cruising the Chesapeake"* by William H. Shellenberger, and *"Chapman Piloting Seamanship & Small Boat Handling"* by Elbert S. Maloney. Of some surprise to the captains and crew was how little reading time was really available to us on the cruise. The days had hardly any "down time", with the efforts of sailing the boats, navigating, servicing the boats, touring, and cooking preoccupying our time.

"One more element remained to be considered, which, if not under the head of comfort, comes under the more important one of health, I mean

cleanliness. Nothing so disturbs rest as the thought that as one sleeps visitors, demons of the night, children of filth, are feasting upon his blood; or that some disease-germ, vigorous in the absence of fumigation, is nursing in his veins a progeny that shall work him unknown harm. This bar to bliss when cruising is often intimately associated with a hired vessel. But then there could be no excuse for it on board one's own yacht, so I determined that, inside and out, the vessel should be cleaned every day. This rule was observed during the entire cruise, save for two weeks very early in the season. The yacht was also pumped out, washed out, and fumigated on the least suspicion that anything might be wrong, or on the bare idea that peace of mind or health of body could be in the least degree sub served by any additional precaution.

And now, -

Over the rail

My hand I trail,

Within the shadow of the sail;

A joy intense,

The cooling sense

Glides down my drowsy indolence. - Drifting.".

CHAPTER II
DOWN THE CHESAPEAKE
AND UP THE JAMES.

Destination: Still Pond, MD
Saturday, June 15, 2013
(28 Nautical Miles, 7 Hours)

Joseph Rothrock entered the Chesapeake Bay on Saturday, June 10, 1883, through the Chesapeake and Delaware Canal in the Upper Bay. On the previous day he had traversed the canal under tow from the steam-tug *Swallow*. He writes of his first day on the Chesapeake, *"On Saturday morning our patience was almost exhausted before we were taken in tow by the tug for the Elk River. The master of the tug did not care to venture out so long as the fog remained dense. Probably he was entirely right, because until eight o'clock objects distant more than a hundred yards were shut out from view; though the captain of a large Crisfield schooner did not think so, and, hoisting his sails, he started to work his way down to the Elk. However, "luck in leisure-,"we passed him very soon when the tug did start.*

As we entered the Elk the fog cleared away entirely, and the glorious water view opened before us to the southward. I never look from above the Bohemian River down toward the bay that this panorama does not impress me. It does so more and more the oftener I look at and enjoy it. To the south there is no visible limit. The bold, timber-covered bluffs east or west, navigable rivers coming in between, run so that the horizon widens as one looks south. It is a scene characterized neither by grandeur nor yet by quiet beauty alone. The combination of water, of plains, and of hills in just the proper proportion is what completes this perfect picture, so perfect, too, that each season brings its own special beauty to the view. Back from the water a little distance, on higher ground, may be seen the comfortable houses of the farmers. Without indicating the presence of great wealth, the whole appearance of the region is one of thrift and abundance. There is no sign of the "take-it-as-it-comes" spirit which is so common south of Annapolis; the air of the place rather speaks, "Make the most of it." Turkey Point, high and timber-clad, the location of an important light-house, stands like a sentinel between the Elk and the wide, shoal mouth of the Susquehanna River.

Probably one should say as little harsh in character about wind or weather as possible when cruising, for he can alter neither one nor the other; neither does it indicate a well-ordered mind to find fault with that which cannot be helped, and which, even if we could alter, would probably be the worse for the interference. Still, as a simple inquiry, it may be allowed us to ask, how many days of the summer season does the southern-bound navigator find head-winds to contend with on the upper, or indeed the whole, Chesapeake Bay?"

Unlike Rothrock, we began our voyage of the Chesapeake from the south, and sailed north up the Bay from the Magothy River. *Second Wind* and *CamiCat* are both berthed on the Magothy. In the months leading up to the voyage both boats had been involved in extensive preparation for the journey, including work on mechanical equipment, navigation systems, and laying in of ship's stores.

As we began our voyage, the ships complement aboard *Second Wind* consisted of Cece, John, Jamie, and myself. Aboard *CamiCat* were Camilla, Nina, Bob, Solveig, and Christer.

CamiCat Departs The Magothy

We departed our dock at 10:30 after a busy morning spent finishing our outfitting and collecting crew that would stay with us through our first weekend. By 11:30 we had completed refueling, pumping out holding tanks, and watering, and had joined up with *CamiCat* to head out the river and up the Bay. Winds were light, 5 to 10 knots, blowing from the east. As the day wore on they would shift to the southeast.

By four in the afternoon we were standing off Pooles Island in the upper Bay. Captain John Smith's 1612 map of the Chesapeake locates the island as "Powels Iles". It was named by Smith after one of his companions during his 1608 explorations of the Bay. By the early 18th century a small settlement occupied the island, which in April 1813 was plundered by the British during the War of 1812. By 1873, seven thousand peach trees had been planted on the island, and the fruit marketed in Baltimore. Such was its state when Rothrock sailed past the island in 1883. But, in 1917, the island was purchased by the Federal Government as part of the establishment of the Aberdeen Proving Grounds, and today the island is off limits to the public, with unexploded ordinance still on the island. As we passed east of the island we saw a military patrol craft sitting off a sandy beach patrolling the island and preventing small private craft from straying too close to the island.

Passage East of Pooles Island

Shortly after passing Pooles Island we passed *Key of Sea*, a Pearson 26 owned by my brother-in-law Patrick and his partner Dan. Patrick had just purchased the boat and was headed down the Bay from North East, Md. Patrick and Dan were driving the boat into the wind with a 9 horsepower outboard, and had not yet reached the halfway point in their voyage. After a quick greeting was exchanged, we continued on to the north. Patrick and Dan would join us again in Solomons Island for the last week of our voyage.

At about five-thirty in the afternoon we headed into Still Pond and our anchorage for the night. We had caught up to *Martha*'s wake, and would spend the next three weeks following Rothrock's journey. Rothrock's entry into Still Pond was recorded with these words, *"By four in the afternoon we entered what is known to fishermen, oystermen, and others of aquatic tastes as Still Pond Harbor. It lies just south of where the Sassafras River empties, or rather opens, into the Chesapeake.*

That which is taken for the harbor generally is but a deep indentation or bay opening to the west, and hence, with a wind from the same direction, is merely a trap from which there can be hardly an escape, and in which one must ride out a sea backed by the width of the bay. In the October gale, some years ago, there were several "oyster-pungies" lost in this very harbor; so, at least, I was informed. I had good reason for knowing that there was one such unfortunate there as late as 1879, for, entering the harbor about dark in the evening with the schooner "Alice M.," we struck fairly upon the wreck, fortunately for us, however, with no evil results. Not a sign the presence of this dangerous obstacle save the "wake" or ripple made by the wreck itself.

The Still Pond is an offshoot or an island prolongation of the harbor, and with which it is connected by an inlet say seventy feet wide and twice or thrice as long. That we found it and came to anchor in it, as but few yachtsmen do, I am indebted entirely to the sagacity and the pluck of "Lew," to whom, by the way, I have not yet introduced the reader.

"Lew" is a comely, open-hearted yachtsman, of say twenty-one, whom I was fortunate enough to secure as assistant before I left the Delaware. He is experienced, companionable, and trustworthy; and I can only hope that in future I may never meet with a worse man or a less reliable man than Lewis Seaman. It was through him, as I have said, that we found the way into Still Pond. I had been in the harbor before, and had not found the pond. He had not been there before, but did find it. That is just the difference. He noticed the inlet and saw how rapidly the tide ran out, and at once reasoned there must be a large body of water behind the inlet to force a current through with such velocity.

So we headed for the inlet, and gradually saw how it increased in size as we approached, until, when in its mouth, the pond opened to our view; but the current, which suggested the pond, well nigh prevented our reaching it. The wind died away as we approached the inlet, and when we were in it, ceased entirely. So the anchor was dropped, and then "Lew," taking a rope over his shoulder, went ashore. I hoisted the anchor on board, and "Lew" towed the yacht through into the mouth of the pond. East and west the landlocked, beautiful pond spread out before us. Everyone who is fond of the water has some ideal harbor which suggests perfect safety, easy landing on attractive shores, and what more each must add for himself to complete the picture. To me, when longing for a week on the water, this one, Still Pond, is ever uppermost in my mind. I often plan a whole vacation spent there. There is room enough for a large fleet in the pond, but, unfortunately, the bar across the mouth prevents vessels drawing more than three feet of water from entering. My chart shows on the southern shore of the harbor another arm, much like this on the north, but I have never explored it. In the interest of humanity, it is to be hoped that means may be taken to deepen the channel into this Still Pond; for it is doubly hard that men should perish, as in that October gale, when there is an absolutely secure anchorage in full sight.

Considered from another stand-point, this place is one of those glorious surprises which so often strike a person cruising in the Chesapeake. Not only did the beauty of the spot take possession of me as soon as it was disclosed, but within half an hour after we had dropped anchor, Lew's net had caught all the fish we needed for supper. Had the Pilgrim Fathers landed here instead of where they did, it is doubtful whether their piety and importance would have allowed them to stop short of the belief that a spot so delightful and so prolific was created especially for them, and the work of Indian extermination might have been prosecuted with intense zeal. Pike, yellow neds, perch, catfish! Surely such a bill of fare might well awaken the enthusiasm of any man with a yachtsman's appetite, even if he were absolutely devoid of his sporting proclivities."

Second Wind Enters Still Pond

Unlike Rothrock, we had the advantage of a well marked channel to follow into Still Pond. We also had a GPS chart-plotter that positioned us exactly. Navigation was clear-cut, and lacked the uncertainty of Rothrock's time. Just past a Coast Guard Station to port, we turned into the fresh water lake. We found the water depths very shallow, but like Rothrock we had the advantage of drawing less than three feet of water. Rothrock's description of the pond was found to be little changed after 130 years, and the beauty of the anchorage has been little marred by time. We passed ospreys, eagles, and blue herons as we came into the pond, and the cameras were quick to try to photograph them all.

Rothrock goes on in his book to reflect that, *"Every hour of day or night appeared to me to have brought some peculiar sound. In the morning we had catbirds, blackbirds, kingfishers, and fish-hawks; at noon, a family of crows, young and old, kept up a most persistent and vigorous cawing. Whether the last was a lesson in elocution for the junior members of the family I cannot say, though there appeared to be some object and some method in it. At night a legion of frogs gave us a prolonged high-toned serenade.*

Close along the northern shore there is a clean, gravelly bottom, and a somewhat greater depth of water than a little farther out, where, on top of the gravel, a slimy, dark, oozy mud is deposited. The tide at that point appeared to flow more rapidly along-shore. Examining the mud microscopically, we found much decaying, loamy matter, some very fine sand, and a number of the siliceous skeletons of diatoms. I never saw so many, or such industrious fish-hawks. All day long we could hear them coming down with a splash into the water. Of course an occasional bald eagle appeared, to exact his contribution from the hawks. Even the crows seem to be unusually aquatic in their habits here. I saw one go down into the water almost as recklessly as the fish-hawks did. High grounds and low grounds were close by our anchorage, and we found the yellow clover, the small verbena, the blue-flag, and the mountain-laurel all within a stone's throw of where we lay."

Anchored in Still Pond Looking Southeast

After anchoring and rafting the boats together, we found ourselves surrounded by a beautiful wooded shoreline. The only significant change we observed from Rothrock's written description of the anchorage was a disappearance of the frogs and their evening serenade. Scientists have been worried about the decline in amphibians for years now, and a recent U.S. Geological Survey (USGS) found that frogs, salamanders, and amphibians of all kinds are disappearing at an annual average rate of 3.7%. At the current rate of decline, these species will disappear from half of the habitats they currently occupy in about 20 years, says the USGS. The disappearance of the frog's high toned serenade was just one of many environmental changes we came to reflect on during the voyage.

Solveig's First Swim

The crews of both boats changed quickly into bathing suits and found the water. Of consequence, Christer and Camilla had brought onboard for the weekend their daughter Nina, her husband Bob, and their 18 month old granddaughter Solveig. Solveig enjoyed her first swim in the Bay, and after initial cries of terror, soon found her father's arms a great comfort. After the swim Nina and Bob cooked supper for both boats. Dinner was a camping dish called "shlop" that in spite of its name and evil look was found to be extremely tasty and satisfying.

Destination: Worton Creek, MD
Sunday, June 16, 2013
(8 Nautical Miles, 2 Hours)

We awoke Sunday to partly cloudy skies and cool temperatures. Like Rothrock's experience, we were encircled by the sound of osprey (fish-hawks), crows and songbirds. Perched in a tree along the shore overlooking the pond was a bald eagle surveying her domain. After a quick consultation between the skippers, we decided on a mid morning departure to try to beat the threat of early afternoon thunderstorms and a Coast Guard "small craft warning". By 9:20 we were underway with 8-10 knot winds building from the south-west.

Osprey Nesting Atop a Channel Marker in Still Pond

Our departure from Still Pond was not as harrowing an experience as that experienced 130 years earlier by Rothrock. He writes *"Monday, the 11th, we were off by six in the morning. It was natural that we should leave Still Pond with regret. We had no reason to anticipate finding other harbors both as safe and as pleasant. Let me say to other yachtsmen that, in going out the inlet, back-flaws and baffling winds may very often, if not usually, be expected as the bluff, where the pond narrows into the inlet, is passed. Sometimes these uncertain elements cause no little trouble in "working ship" where the channel is so narrow."*

Still Pond Channel

Three advances of time simplified our departure from the inlet. First was the introduction of navigation aids by the U.S. Lighthouse Service which in 1939 was incorporated into the U.S. Coast Guard. A slow evolution in the types and placement of buoys and lights in waters of the United States has made navigating far less dangerous than Rothrock experienced in 1883. This system employs a simple arrangement of colors, shapes, numbers and light characteristics to mark navigable channels, waterways and adjacent obstructions. Second, the dredging of Still Pond channel envisioned by Rothrock has been accomplished and small boats today have seven feet of water at the entrance to the pond. Finally, the internal combustion engine which now provides auxiliary power to most small cruising sailboats eliminates the risk of "backflaws and baffling winds" by simply allowing the boater to power through them.

Our departure from the pond was however challenged by a different obstacle, and that was the crab pots and their floats. Working our way through the channel, we soon moved into fields of floats that had to be dodged with the same skill as playing a video game. The call came out from crew "to port" or "to starboard", and quick maneuvers took us steadily past progressive rows of pots. This exercise was one repeated many times as we worked our way down the Bay in the following days.

About half a mile offshore we spotted a bald eagle working its way into the Bay with purpose. We followed the bird in its flight until it dove with firm determination into the water to grasp a large fish. It turned back toward land and struggled back to shore with its massive catch.

Rothrock's original goal for the day was to sail into Annapolis, but adverse wind and tide soon turned him into Worton Creek. He writes, *"Once out in the bay the little "Martha" encountered the full force of a strong head-wind, and fairly danced on the waves like a cork. Whitecaps were forming on all sides. The wind was puffy and uncertain, now almost a calm, when the boat would lose her headway and lie like a log; then in an instant a violent puff would strike the sail, knocking the yacht down, rail to the water, before she could gather speed enough to make her mind the helm. We now appreciated the full value of the fixed iron ballast. More would have been better, as the excessive buoyancy was a disadvantage in these short, chopping seas. Ballasted, as the boat had been the previous year, with sand, most of which was hardly below the water-line, such sailing must have been dangerous in the extreme. The amazing stupidity of many yacht owners is absolutely a marvel. Most of those with whom I spoke before placing the iron in my vessel were rather inclined to tender their sympathy that I could be stupid enough to buy iron when I could pick up sand or stones. The reason why I did not buy more and place it where it belonged, outside in the form of an iron keel, was because it involved an expense greater than I felt at liberty to incur. The worst fault was not lack of stiffness, but great buoyancy. Lew remarked, in a quiet way, "This boat takes the trouble to go right over the tops of all these waves." So it was; for sometimes she actually appeared to jump half her length out of the water. Three miles ahead we sighted another point, one which marked a tempting harbor. The tide had turned and was against us; this, with adverse winds and waves, decided us to put into the harbor, Worton's Creek. The attempt to beat down to Annapolis involved a long, hard day's work, with no pleasure whatever in the sail. Giving the yacht more sheet, we headed for the creek, entering it in good style, flying past a party of fishermen who were running out an immensely long seine. Once fairly in, we sighted two arms, one of which ran northward, opening into a considerable expanse of water, the other and more inviting one extending toward the south. We beat into the latter about a mile, and dropped our anchor opposite to Buck Neck Landing. Shortly afterward the steamer "Van Corlear," from Baltimore, came in and afforded us a chance to send off our mail."*

Worton Creek Anchorage

At mid day we came into Worton Creek, to be greeted by the sight of several large marinas along the shore. Moving up the creek, we dropped anchor in seven feet of water where Mill Creek intersects Worton Creek. Anchored, we looked to shore where Buck's Neck Landing is now home to Worton Creek Marina. The view along the creek would have been unrecognizable to Rothrock, as now marinas and boats dominate the scenery. A quick trip ashore had us conversing with yacht owners and live-a-boards. One older couple of interest was living aboard a houseboat that had once been part of a fleet of houseboats they had kept in commercial charter at the marina. The high cost of fuel and the downturn in the economy had eroded the business, and they had moved onto the last of their houseboats in retirement, selling off the rest of the fleet. They complained that a three and a half hour run into Baltimore could burn 60 gallons of fuel at a cost that made it cheaper to drive around the Bay and rent a hotel room in the city than pay the high fuel costs of a boat.

Of his stay in the creek Rothrock wrote, *"For a while the place appeared to be alive, carriages thronging the wharves to receive those coming, and to help away those who were leaving. But they departed with the steamer, and in half an hour the place resumed its wonted quietness. Dreaminess appeared to rule the hours. For the rest of the day hardly a sign of life was visible. I made several attempts to purchase some rope which I needed on the yacht, but found the merchant was taking a nap, or had gone visiting, or was somewhere else than in his store. Late in the evening the desired purchase was made. The law of compensation, it is evident, runs through the whole universe outside of ourselves. I am convinced now that it at last decides the individual destiny. Were it not for some such law, men at Buck Neck Landing might live forever, or certainly as long as the patriarchs. The world's troubles do not appear to concern them, the world's thoughts never agitate them; come peace, come war, nerve-tissues and myosin are renewed as fast as expended, and but for some beneficent disease or accident men never would leave there to stay even in Paradise. The place would be overcrowded. With fish in the waters and fruit on the land, these kind-hearted, generous, and honest inhabitants would remain, in quiet and in sunshine, until they multiplied enough to wear their clothing out by jostling against each other.*

There was a solitary living exception to what I have said, visible from meridian until four P.M. A good-natured colored boy amused himself by the hour sculling a heavy "yawl-boat" over to the western side of the creek; then, hoisting a broad board in the bow for a sail, he threw himself down in the stern of the boat and scudded before the wind back to the eastern shore. He was full of the languid poetry of drifting; his whole soul was saturated with it, though it never found expression. The solitary reader of his Muse was myself. Happiness is a purely relative term. This, of course, is a platitude. But who of all mankind ever come to fully appreciate the breadth of even so plain a thing, and to rest content with the present? I have in mind now two who illustrate the extremes. One of them is that young negro. He came alongside, and I gave him a bucket of preserved prunes, which neither Lew nor myself could tolerate. He received them with open eyes and mouth. If he only knew how little generosity there was in that gift, we would suffer in his estimate. He soon became too full of happiness on preserved prunes even to enjoy the pleasure of crossing the creek behind his board-sail. We saw him on the other side, with his feet hanging over the boat and receiving the caress of the water, just as his face, upturned to the sun, was comforted by the superheated rays. An hour later Pompey came alongside again. For the gift of a cigar he consented to have his "picture tuk.

Marked on the lower part of the store building I found the statement, "High-water mark. September 17, 1876." It was gratifying to obtain the fact, not only because it was a fact and indicated a storm-tide several feet higher than common, but because it evinced interest in an unusual event. However, two months later I should have seen busy times on that very quiet wharf, when the peach crop, one great interest of the region, was being shipped. We went ashore during the evening, and enjoyed the hospitality and conversation of one of the near residents."

Ryana at Anchor

Coming back to the *Second Wind* from our shore excursion, we ran across Ryan and Diana who were returning back to their 40 foot sailboat *Ryana*. They had just finished walking their dog Stanley ashore and were circling our rafted boats in their dinghy. Like us, they also owned a catamaran. They were interested in the design and sailing abilities of our Island Packet Cats. A quick invitation to tour our boats turned into a drink, and we sat in the cockpit and listened to their tale. They were leaving jobs and the "material world" behind and were taking a two-year sabbatical aboard their new boat, a Lagoon. They had left the west coast and their jobs in April, picked up their boat in North Carolina, and were headed north. The last two months they had slowly worked into the Chesapeake as they tried to keep up with a myriad of equipment and system failures in the boat. It was something Ryan never expected from a new production boat. Ryan's frustration with poor boatyard repairs was leading him to try to manage as many on board repairs as he could to avoid "lousy workmanship". They were headed to Maine and from there south again to the Caribbean. Their enthusiasm for adventure was wonderful to hear, though Diana made it clear that she was not "camping" on her Lagoon and intended to enjoy some comforts in the adventure. They later provided their own tour of *Ryana* for Bob and Nina.

The Fishing Expedition

After lunch *CamiCat*'s dinghy was back in the water again, taking Bob and Nina on a fishing expedition. A few minutes later *Second Wind's* dinghy set off on a second mission to explore Mill Creek. Both expeditions proved successful. The fishing expedition caught six perch to serve as appetizers before supper. Cooked wonderfully with dill, they were consumed to great acclaim and in great haste.

The Mill Creek expedition rowed back after running out of fuel with reports of a sea plane tied up along shore. This discovery generated a second trip by Christer and John to investigate the airplane, it turned out to be a Searey kit airplane that is now manufactured in Florida by Progressive Aerodyne. A two-man amphibious aircraft, the plane mounts a single engine above the wings, and drives a single rear-facing pusher propeller. Of all the transformations observed in *Martha's* wake, the lone amphibious plane sitting on the dock upstream of the old steamer landing at Buck's Neck Landing best illustrates how far transportation has advanced in one hundred and thirty years.

Perch Ready for the Grill

At 10:45 in the evening, Jamie, who had joined us for just two days, departed company. She was picked up at the marina to return to a normal workweek. This was the first of numerous crew changes to be made over the next three weeks.

Destination: Annapolis, MD
Monday, June 17, 2013
(29.4 Nautical Miles, 6.5 hours)

With a new morning, Christer rose early to fly his aerial drone and photograph the creek. Water spray from landing broke the electronics in the digital camera, but the pictures were saved. Later he mounted a second camera to allow a continuation of his aerial photography.

Buck's Neck Landing

Like Rothrock, our objective for the day was to sail down the Bay to Annapolis. Rothrock wrote of the day, *"Tuesday, the 12th, we left our anchorage on the last of the ebb tide, and headed south for Annapolis. We hoped by making an early start to reach our destination in spite of the adverse and heavy weather. So we did, but it was at the cost of vast patience and severe buffeting. As the crow flies, the distance would have been considerably less than thirty miles. In a fair wind the run would have been a very short one; but in a small boat, with wind and tide both against us, it consumed a great part of the day. Yet it appeared that we were not much "worse off than others who were in sight and bound the same way. Harbor after harbor was passed, until by two o'clock P.M. it was clear that, even with the odds against us, reaching our destination was merely a question of time and perseverance. Hoping to avoid the force of the waves, we left the eastern shore and started for the other side. To my surprise, where I expected to find a sheltered shore, the water was almost or quite as rough as the one we had left. The difference in color between the deep-green water and the yellowish hue in shoaler places was strikingly apparent. From Bodkin Point, down along the western shore, the beat appeared almost interminable. We had fully decided at one time on anchoring in Magothy Harbor. On mature reflection we both concluded it would be just a little unmanly to remain there over-night, when a friend and prospective shipmate was waiting for us in Annapolis."*

Our departure from Worton Creek proved to be a chaotic affair when anchor lines crossed between *CamiCat* and *Second Wind*. The effort of uncrossing anchors and chains proved nothing less than bedlam as the boats slowly drifted into the shallows and two boat hooks went overboard. After 20 minutes of orders and counter orders, the anchors were finally sorted out and we were underway. The winds had swung to the southwest and intensified throughout the day as we approached Sandy Point Shoal Light, and like Rothrock, we spent the day beating against the wind as it intensified.

Just before passing under the Bay Bridges we passed the Sandy Point Shoal Light. Construction of the lighthouse was started in late August 1883, about a month after Rothrock left the Bay on his summer cruise. An earlier lighthouse and keeper's house had been constructed on shore at about the same location where the Bay Bridge now crosses the shoreline. But this earlier lighthouse provided little assistance to fog-bound steamships traversing up and down the Bay in the mid 1800's. In August 1882, Congress authorized $25,000 for the construction of a new lighthouse to be built upon the shoal. One year later, a contractor and crew started work on a platform that would allow them to set in place and sink a caisson as a foundation for the new lighthouse. The caisson was sunk 3 feet into sandy bottom, was filled with concrete, and a 2 ½ story brick octagonal tower was built of masonry to house the light keeper, light, and fog horn. The lighthouse went into service in October 1883, and has serviced marine traffic into Baltimore ever since.

Annapolis

We beat past the light and finally motored under the Chesapeake Bay Bridge in mid afternoon as the winds continued to build and a thunderstorm formed and moved across the Bay just south of us. John had the helm most of the afternoon, and was to learn valuable lessons about our catamarans lack of ability to "point and foot" to windward.

Rothrock's reflections of his sail into Annapolis were these: *"It did appear, though, as if we never could get by Sandy Point. It shoals a long, long way out. Then, too, fellow-yachtsmen, be advised : do not attempt, as we did, to go inside of the buoys off Greenbury Light when it is blowing a gale, unless you know the ground too well to make a mistake. The "Martha" tried the experiment, and, though she did drag over, there was nothing at all to spare. It is very trying to keep outside, especially when the wind is against you, but probably you will find it best to do so.*

We received a lesson in naval architecture when crossing from the eastern to the western shore. My boat, being the usual model of the Delaware Bay, broad and short, was at her very worst in the head-wind and "choppy sea" of the Chesapeake. She labored severely, with lee rail under (for we were carrying whole sail, though the wind whistled through the rigging), or rose over the waves until it appeared as if more than half the hull was out of water. Alongside of us came a Chesapeake "bug-eye,"* of light draught, but long and narrow. We saw her start from Tolchester Beach, and creep up on us swiftly and surely. We were laboring; she was moving along without effort, going not only faster, but working more to the windward. At the very time this forty-foot bug-eye was leaving us, we ourselves were distancing a large coasting schooner. The bug-eye careened over very little, went easily through the water, made no pounding or splashing, and looked almost into the wind. Thus she proved herself as possessing every requisite of a first-class sea-goer. It is doubtful if she drew more than two feet and a half of water; it is much more probable that she drew less. She certainly did not have ballast enough to sink her if she had filled with water. These were all most desirable features in a small boat. But here was a direct violation of what we have been taught were cardinal features in small-boat construction, shallowness and small beam on the one hand, and great length, with no ballast, and shallowness on the other. The present ruling *fashion is that a small boat shall be at least four times as long as broad, and that she shall carry, say, half her tonnage, or more, deep down in the water, in the shape of a lead or iron keel. It is certain that a boat built after this, the English cutter model, may "knock down;" but it is certain she will not stay down. Unless she fills, she must right again. I believe that, so far as our American sloop and the English cutter have come into fair trial, the cutter has proven the better boat, safer and faster. I am not sure what the result of a contest between the cutter and the bug-eye would be. From what I have seen of the latter class of boats in the Chesapeake, I am most strongly prepossessed in their favor. The model of this nondescript is peculiar. Probably the light cedar gunning-skiff which does duty as a yawl-boat for us is as nearly an exact mutation of the bug-eye model as one can imagine. Now, that same skiff, with sharp bow and stern, such as the bug-eye was, gave us, when we towed it down to Annapolis through heavy seas, a most astonishing illustration of seaworthiness. Every vessel we met had her yawl swung up, or on deck. Yet our yawl rode so easily that the line by which we towed her was seldom stretched, and not a tin-cupful of water worked into her during the whole day."*

By 4:00 in the afternoon we had picked up a mooring off the U.S. Naval Academy. A short time later the harbor master came out in his small boat to collect mooring fees. He turned out to be a young ex-marine who was out of service on a medical discharge after serving three tours of duty in Afghanistan. Like Rothrock, 130 years ago, we still live with war, its aftermath, and the cruel pain it brings to both the soldier and society. Today America welcomes back thousands of young veterans from service and wounded soldiers from Afghanistan and Iraq, many on medical discharges like the young harbor master. One hundred thirty years ago the faces were the same, but the war was different. The ex-marine was rebuilding a life after the horrors of war, and in this not much has changed over time.

Rothrock goes on to write of his Annapolis visit, *"A day could not be spared, on our way down, to see the points of interest in and about Annapolis without a serious break in our plans. However, as we found a friend (Lieutenant Bull, of the navy), the break was made, and the time spent in the grounds of the Naval Academy, under his guidance, was a more than sufficient compensation for waiting."*

Annapolis City Dock

As it appears today, the Academy would be unrecognizable to Rothrock. The only structure now standing on the Academy grounds that existed in 1883 is the Maryland Avenue Gatehouse.

The Naval Academy was established in 1845 on the site of the Army's former Fort Severn. First opened as a Naval School in 1850, the Academy initiated a four year consecutive course of study with summer cruises introduced to provide practical seamanship experience to young midshipmen. During the Civil War years of 1861 to 1865, the Academy relocated to Newport, Rhode Island, and the Academy grounds were used as a military hospital and encampment. By 1883 when Rothrock visited, the Academy had been eighteen years back in Annapolis with a course of study that required six years to complete. The last two years were spent at sea as final preparation for a young midshipman's military career.

The Spanish American War in 1898 won for the Navy and the Academy national recognition. What followed was a general expansion of both the Navy and the Academy. New construction, beginning in 1899, resulted in a complete rebuild of the Academy. Bancroft Hall, completed in 1901, stands today at the center of the academy and houses approximately 4,300 midshipmen. More than 200 major buildings occupying over 245 acres of land have been built since 1899. The academy grounds today serve to educate young men and women in preparation for careers of military service.

Water taxis run from the Annapolis mooring fields to various locations along the waterfront during summer months. We caught one of these boats ashore to deposit Bob, Nina, Solveig and John who had all finished their part of the cruise. After landing ashore and enjoying a brisk walk, we found ourselves at Davis Tavern in Eastport. The tavern is a local sailor's bar, and we found ourselves in a corner table celebrating a successful start to the cruise. Family and friends joined us, and we parted company in fine revelry after more than one toast was drunk.

Celebrating in Davis Tavern

Destination: Smith Creek, MD
Tuesday, June 18 to Wednesday, June 19, 2013
(70.3 Nautical Miles, 11 Hours)

Wind and weather had built through the night, and by Tuesday morning the skies were overcast with a forecast for heavy rain behind a cold front that was moving through. After a consultation between skippers, it was decided to remain in Annapolis another day to allow the bad weather to pass. We decided to refuel the boats and move to a more protected anchorage on Back Creek. By 10 in the morning we were settled in at our new moorings with light rain falling when the Harbor Master approached to check ships' documents. He was following up in a search for a sailboat that U.S. Customs was trying to locate on the Bay. Our imaginations ran wild over the general cause for such a search, but no clue was given by the Harbor Master as to the real story behind the investigation.

Back Creek Looking East onto the Bay

A heavy afternoon deluge with reported tornados located not far from us at Baltimore Washington International Airport justified the wisdom of our staying in port. The crews, now made up of Christer, Camilla, Cece and myself, rested and played board games throughout the storms.

Wednesday morning the skippers woke early planning for a 5:30 departure. The wind had swung from the north behind the cold front, and a steady wind and an outgoing tide carried us quickly out the Severn River and into the Bay.

Rothrock's departure from Annapolis mirrored our own as he wrote, *"When we left, on the morning of the 14th, we were comforted by the assurance, received the day before, that we might expect head-winds going down the bay about nine days out of ten at that season. However, thanks to the squall of the previous evening, the wind had hauled around to the north, and we had a fresh breeze following us all day. So that, after a run of ninety miles, we dropped our anchor for the night in Smith's Creek, a little offshoot from the Potomac. The small number of sails we saw in making the run was a surprise, bearing no comparison to what we expected, or to what we should certainly have seen had we been on the Delaware. Still, it is hard to think that Baltimore, with its superb water approaches, will long lag in the race.*

Chesapeake Bay Bridge at Sunrise

By 7:00 in the morning we were off Highland Beach, on the western shore of the Bay. With binoculars in hand, we were looking for the Douglas Summer House. This home, facing the waterfront just north of the South River, was finished in 1895, twelve years after Rothrock's cruise. Fredrick Douglas, the famed African American statesman, orator, and writer, was 76 years old when his son, Major Charles Douglas, developed the Highland Beach subdivision as an African American beach resort and community. Fredrick Douglas had the house built, but never lived to see it finished. Tradition records that Fredrick Douglas designed the house himself with a second floor balcony sighted to look across the Chesapeake to the Eastern Shore where Douglas had been born into slavery. The Highland Beach community became an African American summer community where some of the most successful post Civil War black leaders visited, including Booker T. Washington, Paul Robeson, Paul Lawrence Dunbar, and Langston Hughes.

Thomas Point Shoal Light

As we approached the mouth of South River we sailed by Thomas

Point Shoal Light. This light was commissioned in November 1875, and was eight years old the summer of Rothrock's cruise. Designed by staff professionals of the U.S. Lighthouse Service, the structure sits in seven feet of water at the mouth of South River. Architecturally one of the most distinctive lighthouses on the Bay, the octagonal wood framed lighthouse was built atop of nine screwpiles attached to iron framing. The lighthouse remains as built with only minor modification.

Wind and tide continued to move us quickly down the Bay at seven knots, past West River, Herring Bay and on to Calvert Cliffs. Shortly after the cliffs, we sighted the Cove Point Liquefied Natural Gas (LNG) terminal. *CamiCat* veered west to take a closer look at the terminal only to be chased by a guard boat that warned the boat away from the complex.

In his job as a naval architect for a large oil company, Christer had visited the Cove Point terminal a few years earlier. His visit was memorable, and he told us this story of the facility:

In the late 1800's the world's energy of choice was wood and coal. The age of liquid hydrocarbon fuels would not materialize until after the development of the internal combustion engine. At the time of Rothrock's voyage this technology was in its infancy. It wasn't until 1872 that the first commercial production of a liquid fueled internal combustion engine occurred. After this date the development and expansion of liquid hydrocarbon fuels would explode. Liquid hydrocarbon fuel quickly took over and became the fuel of choice for heating, transportation and industry. Oil became the liquid gold, and with more oil discoveries, more natural gas was also found in the oil wells. Crude oil was refined into many types of liquid fuels, but the gas was an unwanted byproduct and it was disposed of by flaring or burning it off.

By the mid 1900's, technology had advanced to the point that natural gas could be liquefied and transported by ship. When natural gas was compressed to 600 times its volume, it became a liquid with an associated temperature of -263 degrees Fahrenheit. As a liquid it became economical to transport LNG by ships. The *SS Methane Princess* became the first LNG Carrier capable of transporting this very cold cryogenic liquid. She was designed and delivered in 1964. This ship carried 34,500 cubic meters of LNG and transported LNG safely for 33 years. She was finally scrapped in 1998.

By the 1990's, America's demand for imported LNG had grown. The most common size of new LNG carriers had increased with this demand to about 145,000 cubic meters. In 2003, dual fuel diesel engines capable of operation using either oil or natural gas were introduced, providing a new solution for LNG carrier propulsion. In addition new larger capacity ships of more than 200,000 cubic meters were on the drawing boards.

In 2006, a large LNG ship construction effort was started to build over 50 new LNG mega ships, each with a cargo capacity of 216,000-266,000 cubic meters, mainly for importing LNG to the USA and Europe. An unprecedented combination of perceived shipping capacity need plus technology development brought forth a total building program of 130 LNG ships representing a massive investment of some $26 billion.

That extraordinary cash investment was only about a third of the predicted investment that the energy industry planned for a worldwide expansion of LNG infrastructure. Recent projections, from wishful to committed, claim $52 billion will be spent in the next five years on building new liquefaction trains with a further $24 billion going for building or upgrading import terminals. When added to the shipbuilding program the total LNG related expenditure amounts to approximately $100 billion. To put that in perspective, it is equivalent to the investment in a previous five-year infrastructure rebuilding effort: post World War II's "Marshall Plan" which concluded in 1951 at a cost equivalent today of about $97 billion.

LNG is considered as a viable energy source for the fast growing need for "clean" energy to produce electricity, heating, and cooling for homes and industry. Seven large LNG terminals have been built in the United States and applications for many additional terminals were filed anticipating a need to import this clean energy source. With gas discoveries in Qatar, Africa, the Arctic and Australia, it is estimated that the world's natural gas reserves exceed those of crude oil. Additional gas is also available in most existing oil wells.

Cove Point LNG Terminal

Cove Point LNG terminal was one of the seven built as an import terminal for LNG, servicing the east coast of the United States. It was designed to handle up to 220 ships per year.

The terminal was constructed approximately one mile off the western shoreline of the Chesapeake, and was connected to the shore facilities and the shore based LNG storage tanks by an underwater tunnel. Christer, during his previous visit to the facility, rode a bicycle back and forth through the tunnel in lieu of walking.

There are seven storage tanks with a total capacity of 413,326 m^3 located at the facility. The storage tanks were clearly visible to us from the water.

Nobody could have predicted however, that all of these large

LNG import terminals in the United States would become obsolete overnight. This has occurred due to the large discoveries of shale gas on the North American continent. Shale gas is stored in rock formations below the ground at depths of 5,000 feet or less Vertical and horizontal drilling into these rock formations in conjunction with hydraulic cracking of the rocks will free the gas that can be then pumped to the surface. In addition to the shale gas, very large gas formations have been discovered in the Gulf of Mexico at depths of 10,000 ft requiring drilling in the sea bottom an additional 2000-4000 ft. Today's technology has made it possible to reclaim the gas, so the United States has now become a *potential exporter* of LNG rather than an *importer*. Seven of the existing LNG terminals in the U.S., including Cove Point, are now in the process of being converted to export terminals.

Cove Point Light

Once past the LNG terminal, the Cove Point Light came into view. The light survives today as the oldest light on Maryland's Chesapeake shoreline. Originally built in 1828 by John Donohoo, it was laid of stone, and is today stuccoed and painted white. It is conical in shape and rises 51 feet above the ground. A light-keeper's house is located immediately west of the lighthouse. In 1883, during the cruise of Joseph Rothrock, the keeper's house was being raised to two stories providing three additional rooms on the second story. The light has been in continuous use since 1828.

Point No Point Light

Our voyage continued at a quick pace, and we soon had passed the mouth of the Patuxent River and sailed on to Point No Point Light. This light is one of four lighthouses built on the Bay in the twentieth century. Work was begun on the light in November 1902, and was finished two and a half years later in April 1905. It had a construction cost of $65 thousand. Completion of the project was set back twice due to major storm damage, once in 1903 when an April storm upset the caisson assembly, and again in 1904 with the destruction of an adjacent pier and equipment. It is one of four caisson-type lights built on the Bay, and in style resembles the Baltimore Light, which had also experienced similar problems with storms disrupting the caisson construction.

Point Lookout Marina

By 4:30 in the afternoon we had arrived at Smith Creek. Rothrock wrote of that harbor, *"The little bay, for such it was, in which we had anchored was completely landlocked and not more than two hundred yards wide; yet it contained water enough for a good-sized vessel. This abundance of superior harbors may be considered as a peculiarity in which the Chesapeake is preeminent. This, along with the navigable waters, estuaries, and rivers intersecting the land in all directions, has in one sense retarded the development of the country, i.e., by making water communication so easy and so extensive, it has so far superseded the necessity for roads. The sailing canoe is the ordinary means of travel from place to place along the shores. This retarding effect was observed even by the early colonial writers."*

After four nights at anchor or on a mooring ball, we decided to find a slip for the night at Point Lookout Marina. Our goal was to hook up power to run our air conditioning systems, recharge our batteries, and find a cold drink.

As the heat of the afternoon was upon us, we set off to the marina restaurant, leaving the boats to cool down with the air conditioners running. The reprieve from the heat of the day was welcome, but the disappointment when we returned to the boats to find neither air conditioning unit working was felt most keenly by Camilla who was suffering terribly from the day's heat. The engineering effort to diagnose and repair the air conditioners was to preoccupy the rest of the trip as we chased a fix that was never realized.

Smith Creek Sunset

After our meal, a mega yacht pulled into Smith Creek and dropped anchor for the evening. It was a massive boat, too big for the marina piers. Her crew had been looking for a meal in the restaurant. Her maneuvers in the small creek entertained us for some time. Shortly afterwards, walked to the end of the pier and enjoyed one of the most beautiful sunsets of the journey. The skies exploded in color as we watched the sun sink below the horizon behind the tree line that bordered the cove. It was a sight that forced an involuntary breath from us all.

Destination: Piankatank River, VA
Thursday, June 20, 2013
(46 Nautical Miles, 8 Hours 19 Minutes)

After topping off our fuel, we departed Point Lookout Marina. We set off at 9:00 with light easterly breezes. Heading southeast under power we set a course for Smith Point Light on the south side of the Potomac River. The current light at Smith Point was finished in July 1897, fourteen years after Rothrock had left the Bay. It was built based on the same plans as the Wolf Trap Lighthouse, located in Virginia a few miles north of Mobjack Bay and the York River, which had been completed three years earlier. Like the Baltimore Light and Point No Point Light, it is also a caisson-type structure. This lighthouse is the eighth light structure to aid mariners in this location. Previous lights included three lighthouses built on Smith Point, three lightships, and two offshore lights. The first lighthouse built on Smith Point was built in 1802 for $9,999. Because the original light was built too close to an eroding bluff, it was rebuilt inland in 1807. By 1828, this second structure again was moved farther inland as the shore eroded. In 1821 a lightship was also stationed three miles off Smith Point to aid mariners in locating the Smith Point Shoal. By 1859 the onshore lighthouse was discontinued. In 1861 a Confederate raid destroyed the lightship which was then replaced in 1862 by a 203 ton brig. In 1868 construction of an offshore screw pile lighthouse had been completed, and it was this light that Rothrock sailed past in 1883. In 1893 this lighthouse was damaged by ice flows, and in 1895 severe ice conditions severed the keeper's cottage and the light from the screw pile foundation and carried it away. A lightship was then again temporarily located at the Smith Point Shoals until the present light was built and lit in 1897.

Smith Point Light

Rothrock writes of his trip down the Bay to the Piankatank, *"June the 15th still gave us, in the morning, a promising northerly wind, and we started out early, hoping to make a big run to the southward that day. It was, however, four P.M. when we reached Milford Haven, on the Piankatank River. Our intention had been to push on down to Mobjack Bay, but the weakening wind warned us to seek a harbor while we could have daylight to do it in. No rule can be regarded as invariable when one's doings depend upon the uncertainties of wind and weather. It was my desire, however, always to be at anchor by three in the afternoon. This allowed a turn on shore to see what could be found, and gave us a chance to take in all the surroundings, and decide what we would do in any emergency which might arise during the night."*

By mid morning we had rounded Smith Point and had hoisted sails. Winds were building and shifting to the east. Again, we had found good boat speed and were reaching quickly down the Bay. We were interrupted mid day by a Naval exercise of air cushioned landing crafts off the Rappahannock River. Four LCAC vehicles were on maneuvers, holding our attention as speed, sea, and sea spray kept us in doubt of their purpose and direction. The hovercrafts would drive in formation at very high speed, stop and reform with apparently different purposes. It made a great, if confusing, show.

LCAC Vehicle on Maneuvers

Once past the Rappahannock, with the seas and wind still building, we turned west into the Piankatank and through a sea of crab traps. Around a spit of land protecting the river, we followed the channel into Fishing Bay. With a strong breeze blowing from the north-east, we dropped anchor along the north shore of the bay adjacent the local yacht club and a children's fleet of Optimist Prams. A more sublime view we were not to witness during our voyage as children darted back and forth in small boats with sun, wind, and scenery in complete harmony. *CamiCat* joined us a short time later after experiencing problems dropping the main sail. We rafted the boats together, and after some small excitement with anchors not holding, we had the barbeque grill out and enjoyed a beautiful evening and supper.

Children's Regatta

Rothrock was to spend his evening on the Piankatank in a different anchorage. He writes, *"Milford Haven is still another of those surprises which constantly greet one yachting along the western shore of the Chesapeake. Now, as elsewhere, we were landlocked for the night. The entrance, which at first appeared too small to admit a vessel, widens out into a broad, deep mouth, and inside the harbor which it leads to a whole fleet of canoes and some good-sized schooners lay. During the evening spent there Mr. J. and Lew occupied themselves catching crabs. Half an hour of the sport was sufficient to cover the deck with vigorous pugnacious specimens, who the night through manifested their excessive vitality by threatening any one audacious enough to leave the cabin in the dark hours. However, this was more than compensated for when we came to enjoy them cooked. There is a difference in flavor of crabs, just as there is in that of oysters; and for both Milford Haven is justly famous. Cape May "goodies," served up with the oysters and crabs, make one even now, after the lapse of several months, remember our anchorage in the Piankatank with feelings of complete satisfaction.*

There was a source of annoyance in our charts. These were all that we could desire out in the deep water, but along-shore, in water where we thought we could go, they gave us no information. The score of little bays and harbors that one "might make," if only his chart would indicate the depth of water or show him the way in, were a constant aggravation, because we knew there were such, and such quiet places, too, as we most desired to enter with camera in hand. Chart-makers, we shoal-water yachtsmen, we owners of very small craft, do beseech you to give the channel and the depth of water into every small harbor in the Chesapeake. Our experience at the mouth of the Potomac was provoking. The chart led us to put in there because of a small safe harbor which was indicated; but we searched in vain for it, and were obliged to make a considerable run out of our way to find a secure anchorage."

ROBERT E. CLARKE

Destination: New Point Comfort, VA
Friday, June 21, 2013
(32.1 Nautical Miles, 6 Hours)

The next morning we awoke to the yacht club's youth out on the water again. It was hard to pull ourselves away from watching the racing, as young children in small prams darted in and around the anchorage.

Heading to the Start Line

But by 10:30, despite our reluctance, we raised our anchors and headed back out the river towards the Bay. One hundred thirty years earlier Rothrock's departure was more exciting as he wrote, *"June 16th found us a stir by sunrise, which this season of the year means by about half-past four. We thought ourselves early risers, but the partridges were up before us, and we could hear their musical whistle from all sides. Is it so that there are early and late risers among our day-birds? It was not until long after the "Bob White" whistle was heard that the crows began to make themselves conspicuously noisy. However, this was Virginia we were in, and it is only within a few years that black folks have dared to speak at all.*

Our anchorage in Milford Haven was on the southern side. The anchor was let go in two fathoms of water, but during the night, swinging with the tide, the yacht had been left stern aground. This accident caused but little delay. We were soon floating, and in less than the length of the yacht were again in the channel, with water enough for a large schooner. Most of these harbors have certain features in common. Thus there is ordinarily a bar at the outlet, where the current of the main body of the water, meeting with that coming from the harbor, causes enough retardation of the water to allow the suspended mineral matters to fall to the bottom. Such, at least, is the explanation which forces itself on my mind. There may be a much better one, however, for aught that I know. Then, again, leading to and from all these harbors, there is a strong current where the inlet or outlet is narrow and the harbor is wide. Hence through this narrow part there must be a rapid current, with great capacity for deepening and eroding the channel. This, in fact, is just what we find, and when by storm or otherwise the channel is closed, this swift current very speedily opens another."

We did not follow Rothrock's shortened route south of Gwynn Island into the Bay. He exited the Piankatank at the south end of Gwynn Island through a passage known as the "Hole in the Wall". Rothrock wrote of this route, *"There is a tortuous, very narrow channel from Milford Haven out to the Bay, in which, by sailing east, we hoped to save important time that would have been lost to have gone out from the north as we came in. A very intelligent colored man, one Richard McKnight, undertook to pilot us through this lower passage. We found him a character, who, between serving during war times as a cook for a Northern general and as a sailor, had gathered quite a fund of information. The use he made of his knowledge as we drifted slowly out was very entertaining. His observations upon the animal life around us were quite acute. As for the fish-hawks and the eagles, he seemed to have been taken into their secrets. Their sounds and movements were familiar to him as those of the little boy who accompanied him. Among other things, he told the local tale as to why the eagle exacted a tribute from the hawk. The former was the earlier inhabitant of the region. When the fish-hawk came, he did not know how to make his nest. This the eagle taught him to do, under promise that the hawk should pay in fish for the instruction. This obligation was disregarded, and the eagle was obliged to take his due by force."*

The "Hole in The Wall" has a reported controlling depth of about 4 feet and is used by small local boats, but is exposed to heavy seas. Without local knowledge, we instead routed ourselves north, preferring safety over the time saved by the riskier channel.

Wolf Trap Light

Winds were from the east at six knots and building as the day matured. After motoring into the Bay, the sails were hoisted and we were soon sailing south past Wolf Trap Light. A need for navigation aid at Wolf Trap Shoal was first recognized by Congress in 1819, and by 1821 a light ship had been stationed just off the spit to aid maritime commerce. In 1861 Confederate insurgents destroyed the lightship, and in 1864 a new lightship occupied the spit and remained in place until 1870 when a screw-pile lighthouse was erected on the shoals. It would have been this light that Rothrock passed on his journey. Ten years after Rothrock's cruise, ice flows on the Chesapeake carried away the screw pile structure. The light-keeper was able to escape the light shortly before the ice tore the structure away by walking across ice to a tugboat icebound on the frozen Bay. A gas-lighted buoy and then a light house tender occupied the shoal until 1894 when the current caisson-style light was erected.

Rothrock wrote of his passage, *"The run of the 16th was a very short one. We anchored for the night behind New Point Comfort. So far as the weather was concerned, we rested well enough, but there was a fish-mill on shore which was most exasperatingly fragrant. It called to mind some passages from "The Tempest,*

ADRIAN. The air breathes upon us here most sweetly.
SEBASTIAN. As if it had lungs, and rotten ones.
ANTONIO. Or, as 'twere perfumed by a fen.

The United States boat "Fish-Hawk" lay in the same place. We could not see just what she was doing, though, of course, she had some mission there, and was accomplishing it in the usual comfortable, leisurely government way."

As we sailed farther down the Bay, we were soon watching bottlenose dolphins flash in and out of the water off our port side. A pod would flash to the surface and dive back underwater under a strong sun and in two-foot waves. Their antics looked more play than survival, but they soon veered away and were gone. An unusually high number of these beautiful mammals have been dying off and washing ashore along the mouth of the Chesapeake and up and down the east coast during the summer. The deaths in July were seven times the historic average according to the National Oceanic and Atmospheric Administration. The discovery led to the declaration of "an unusual mortality event" freeing federal resources to investigate. Once again a concern about environmental change, global warming, and the extensive pollution of the Bay raised concerns about the Bay's future and its health. A fear persists that man's poor stewardship is destroying something very precious.

New Point Comfort Light

We continued our steady progress south, and were soon at the mouth of Mobjack Bay. At the intersection of Mobjack and Chesapeake Bays we passed the same New Point Comfort Light that Rothrock anchored off. When this light was originally finished in 1805 the lighthouse stood at the end of a long peninsula that has since eroded into the Bay. Today the lighthouse sits on a small granite rubble island. The lighthouse is a tapered octagonal sandstone structure that was originally built with a keepers house built adjacent to the light tower. The light and keepers house would have been visible to Rothrock as he anchored behind the point that

Saturday evening in 1883. In 1963 a new offshore light was installed by the Coast Guard and the lighthouse abandoned. It stands sentinel today as a day beacon only.

Severn River Looking West

We chose not to anchor off the light, but instead headed across Mobjack Bay to the Severn River which provided a more protected anchorage. The river lacked the high cliffs and hardwood trees we were used to in the northern Bay, and its beauty was not as familiar or scenic as in the upper Bay. Low dank pools lined with thick rushes framed by tall scrub pines defined the shoreline. Herons fishing the edges of the marsh completed the picture.

We anchored at 4:30 in the afternoon, but in our distraction with the shoreline we had failed to shorten the painter on the dinghy. As the anchor set, Cece reversed the engines to set the anchor only to discover the dinghy painter wrapping around our propeller. In the bedlam of engine warning lights and loud alarms sounding, our dinghy was being sucked under the boat. I then put my foot through an open port hatch as I rushed to the stern to help. Adding to the chaos, blood was flowing in some quantity down my leg into the boat through damaged screens. It was not our finest moment. But the chaos was sorted out, and Christer was soon alongside and outfitted in his dive suit to dive and free the propeller.

June 21st marks the summer solstice, and is celebrated in Christer and Camilla's native country of Finland as one of the greatest festivals of the year. In the day's honor, they hosted a Midsummer's Eve celebration complete with schnapps, three types of pickled herring, and Finnish drinking songs. Cece, who was most reluctant to eat herring, was persuaded to try after a few toasts were downed, and bravely put away the slimy fish on a cracker. For this act of bravery she was later awarded a carved fish trophy in recognition of her pluck.

Destination: Fort Monroe, VA
Saturday, June 22, 2013
(27.4 Nautical Miles, 5 Hours 45 Minutes)

We were up early for our final day's sail down the Bay. Our destination was Fort Monroe where we had a late afternoon crew change planned. Karl and Lucia were set to join us aboard *Second Wind*, and Steve and Dee would join *CamiCat* as crew for the James River portion of the cruise.

Land's End Plantation

Departing at 7:45 in the morning, we powered past a historic home named Lands End. The home is located near the southeastern tip of Robins Neck overlooking the Severn River. The plantation house was built between 1796 and 1800 for John Sinclair, a Revolutionary War sea captain. Sinclair is said to have had several occupations in his lifetime. Among these, he is remembered as a ship owner, merchant, ship captain, privateer, privateer agent, ship chandler, naval officer, farmer, and landholding entrepreneur. In these roles he has been judged an enterprising leader, patriot, opportunist, charlatan and anarchist. Sinclair was active during the Revolution as a privateer who served America by conducting dangerous wartime trade with the Caribbean. He famously carried dispatches to French Admiral de Barres whose fleet was stationed in Newport, Rhode Island. Sinclair's action made possible the rendezvous of colonial and French fleets in October 1781 off Yorktown, Virginia, thus forcing the surrender of Lord Cornwallis and the British forces. This British defeat at Yorktown effectively ended the war, although a formal peace treaty took another two years to be signed. Fifteen years after these events Sinclair built Lands End where he lived until his death in 1820. Because the site around Lands End is low and marshy, the home was built with its basement above grade. This provides a distinctive height to the home which is unusual for tidewater plantation homes of its period.

Camilla Takes the Helm

Our day's sail south enjoyed moderate easterly breezes. We sailed from Mobjack Bay past the mouth of the York River, then south towards the Thimble Shoal Light. Lighthouses at this site were some of the most accident prone ever built, and the light today stands as a testament to the dangers intrinsic to lighthouse keeping. The first light at Thimble Shoal was built in 1871, and replaced an earlier lightship anchored at the shoals. In 1880 a fire destroyed this screw pile lighthouse. A replacement structure was quickly rebuilt on the site. This structure would have been the marker that Rothrock passed on his Sunday passage. In 1891 this lighthouse was rammed by a steamer, significantly damaging the structure. Later a coal barge again rammed the lighthouse and damaged the structure. Finally, in 1909, the schooner *Malcolm Baxter Jr.*, which was under tow, rammed the lighthouse and started a fire that completely destroyed the structure. Congress appropriated $68,000 for the reestablishment of the light, and in 1912 Congress appropriated an additional $39,000 for the light. On December 1, 1914, the lighthouse was placed into operation. In 2005 the light was sold at auction, but remains an active aid to navigation.

Passing Thimble Shoal Light

These words captured Rothrock's   sail south into Hampton: *"Sunday morning, the 17th, the wind was so fair that we concluded to start for Fortress Monroe.   An hour before sunrise everything looked unpromising. The wind was not only dead ahead, but there was too much of it. Any other place was better than where we were. It was certain that we must make a harbor somewhere else. Then, too, the Sabbath in full reach of the odors from a fish-mill! It would have been enough to banish all proper feeling, and to concentrate all one's attention on his nose. So the start was made, and soon, as the old adverse breeze died away, a new and favoring one sprang up. This carried us to the fort by half-past two in the afternoon."*

Fort Monroe

From Thimble Shoals we steered east as the winds and seas built and we set a course for Hampton Roads and Fort Monroe. Fort Monroe was built between the years 1819 and 1834, and is sited at the entrance to Hampton Roads at the mouth of the James River. It was designed under the direction of Simon Bernard, a former aide to

Napoleon I. It was built as a part of a larger U.S. coastal defense system that Bernard oversaw in planning. The fort stands as the largest ever built in America, covering over 63 acres of land. It is seven sided in design with walls that are twelve feet high and ten feet thick at the base. The fort mounted between 380 and 412 guns during its nineteenth century service. By 1825 the fort housed ten percent of all U.S. troops and a third of all U.S. artillery. Its history is tied to some of America's greatest historical events and figures, including Edgar Allen Poe and Robert E. Lee, who both served here as young men. Chief Black Hawk was taken to the fort after the Black Hawk Wars of 1832. On March 9, 1862, the fort provided soldiers and visitors a platform to watch the first naval battle of ironclads as the Confederate ship *Merrimack* and the U.S. ship *Monitor* engaged in a battle in Hampton Roads that terminated in a draw. General McClellan launched his great peninsular campaign from the fort in 1862. Abraham Lincoln, U.S. Grant, and the North's leading generals all passed through the grounds in their conduct of the Civil War. Lincoln met with Confederate commissioners for an informal peace conference in the fort in February 1865. With the war's end, Jefferson Davis, president of the Confederacy, was imprisoned in the fort for two years. The fort was decommissioned in September 2011, and in November of 2011, the property was designated a National Monument by President Obama.

The Old Fort Walls

The fort is currently under the stewardship of the Fort Monroe Federal Area Development Authority (FMFADA) which was established as a public body corporate and as a political subdivision of the Commonwealth of Virginia to serve as the official Local Redevelopment Authority. The task of the FMFADA commission is to study, plan, and recommend the best use of the decommissioned military installation.

Rothrock reflected on the area 130 years earlier" *"Hampton Roads and the region around is the veritable historic centre of the country. An accident gave the name, Point Comfort, to the sandy point where Fortress Monroe now stands. Driven by a heavy storm in July from the Piankatank, Captain John Smith found his first secure shelter under its protection. Hence the name, inspired by gratitude. But how often since has the same safe anchorage awakened similar emotions!*

Old Point Comfort Light

The plans for French naval co-operation during the Revolutionary struggle were made here before the advance on Yorktown. In 1813, after being repulsed at Norfolk, the British vented their rage upon the unprotected village of Hampton. During our recent war the possession of Fortress Monroe decided in our favor most important events. Indeed, it is hard to say what might have followed had this position fallen into the hands of our adversaries. A glance at the map will show at once how essential to us it was. There might have been no iron-clad engagement at Newport News, but, instead, Washington and Baltimore would have been exposed to immediate attack from the "Merrimac." Here the first slaves were landed; and in Fortress Monroe was issued General Butler's famous order which declared slaves to be, as property, "contraband of war," an order that removed the curse under which for two centuries the African race had groaned on our free shores.

Fort Monroe Quarters

To speak of that marvel of hotels, the "Hygeia"(under the very guns of Fortress Monroe), is simply to repeat what is already well known.

In the village of Hampton is St. John's Church, one of the ecclesiastical landmarks of the country. It was built in 1658, was in ruins during the war of 1812, and used then by the British as a stable, and burned in 1861, when General Magruder fired the town to prevent its being used by the Northern troops. The walls are built of bricks made in England, and seem as though they might still outlast the centuries, notwithstanding the trials they have endured. I am indebted to the present rector, Rev. J. J. Gravatt, for a photograph, showing one of its sides, in front of which is a group of Indian students from the Hampton School.

So much of history of the early and the late events of national life can seldom be found crowded into so limited an area. Yet I have only alluded to some of the striking outlines of all that has been witnessed here."

Like many Americans, my family also has ties to Fort Monroe. It is where my ancestor, Sgt. William Palmer Clarke, died in service to the Union in August 1862. He is buried today in Hampton National Cemetery under a gravestone that misspells his name. William was the older brother of my great grandfather, and served in the 8th Regiment, Company G, Connecticut Volunteers. Three months after the start of the Civil War, Union forces marched against the Confederate capital of Richmond, expecting to bring an early end to the South's rebellion. On July 21, 1861, Union and Confederate forces met along Bull Run Creek outside Manassas, Virginia. After a major engagement, Union forces were defeated and thrown back to Washington. The North was shocked by the defeat, when an easy victory had been widely anticipated. The U.S. Government realized from the defeat that the war would be longer and more brutal than they had first imagined. On July 22, 1861 President Lincoln signed a bill that provided for the enlistment of half a million men for up to three years of service. In response, William Clarke's regiment was one of three called up in Connecticut by the Governor.

William's Grave

The 8th Regiment Connecticut Volunteers organized in Hartford CT, on September 21, 1861. By mid October 1861, the regiment had deployed to Annapolis, MD, where they remained until January 6, 1862. Moving south down the Bay, the same journey we make now, they joined Burnside's expedition to Hatteras Inlet and Roanoke Island, N.C. They engaged in the Battle of Roanoke Island on February 8, 1862. Remaining on Roanoke Island until March 11th, they then moved to North Carolina, where on March 14 they participated in the Battle of New Berne. They then engaged in operations against Fort Macon between March 23 and April 26, 1862. After the fort's surrender, the regiment remained in New Berne until July, then moved to Newport News, VA. Williams's service lasted ten months, nineteen days. He was 21 years, 8 months, 21 days old as recorded in my grandmother's family papers when he died.

On November 19, 1863, Abraham Lincoln would speak in Gettysburg, Pennsylvania, about the sacrifice made by William and hundreds of thousands of others saying, "that from these honored dead we take increased devotion to that cause for which they gave the last full measure of devotion—that we here highly resolve that these dead shall not have died in vain—that this nation, under God, shall have a new birth of freedom—and that government of the people, by the people, for the people, shall not perish from the earth."

Four million human beings were freed from slavery in the aftermath of the great cause William died for. It would take another one hundred years before the rights of citizenship would be fully bestowed to all the children of slavery.

Quarters 1 – Built 1819

Destination: Jamestown Island, VA
Monday, June 24, 2013
(30.3 Nautical Miles, 7 Hours 30 Minutes)

We departed Old Point Comfort Marina at 8:30 on Monday morning with moderate southerly winds. We ran the boats up the Hampton River into Hampton to refuel. An hour later we were again underway, setting a course southwest through Hampton Roads along the Hampton Flats before turning northwest into the James River and running along the shipyards and marine terminals that define the Newport News waterfront.

Newport News Shipbuilding

The Newport News shipbuilding industry centers itself on large Navy contracts. As we passed the Huntington Ingalls Industry Shipyard we saw the super-carriers *USS Gerald R. Ford* and the *USS*

John F. Kennedy in dry-dock as work progresses to commission them into the U.S. fleet later this decade. The contract cost of the *USS Gerald Ford* is $13.5 billion, and her planned complement of crew will count over 4,600 sailors when she first sees duty in 2016, replacing the *USS Enterprise* which ended her 51 years of sea duty in December 2012.

Rothrock's reflections of Newport News were that *"Northern energy and capital had "taken hold," and many "modern houses" were contemplated, if not actually contracted for. Most of the buildings erected when we were there were of the class that suggested the name "Shanty-town" naturally enough. Their temporary character, the inmates, and the proportion of bar-rooms were strong reminders of some new Western towns I had seen; but, like them, Newport News bids fair to grow into something better. The push and energy of the new West, however, were in striking contrast when placed alongside of the ways of the old South. It is strange indeed that this, the first river region of the continent actually settled in by an English-speaking population, should be about the last to feel the awakening of a real active life. Were I a young man seeking a home, with the privilege of choosing between the West and the James River region, I should decide in favor of the latter. I offer no advice to others in this matter, but what I have written represents my own views upon the subject. I make the statement, too, with a full knowledge of the unhealthfulness of the region; but remember, at the same time (leaving Indiana, Illinois, and portions of Ohio out of the question), that the Juniata Valley of this State (Pennsylvania) was once as bad as the valley of the James is to-day.*

The name Newport News is still full of stirring memories. For one short day the victory gained by the "Merrimac"("Virginia") awakened hopes among the Confederates which must have been bright, the more so as all that had been expected of the new ironclad was far more than realized in her combat with our wooden vessels. These hopes were but bright illusions, for the very next day the "Monitor" turned the tide of victory against the soldiers and the sailors of the South.

Besides the memorable naval battle associated with Newport News, it and the whole northern shore were closely connected with our campaigns against Richmond; just as Norfolk and the southern shore were with the defensive operations going on at the same time on the part of the Confederates."

Second Wind Approaching James River Bridge

Past Hampton Roads we approached the James River Bridge. The original two lane bridge at this site was completed in 1928, forty-five years after Rothrock's voyage and six years after his death. When it was completed, its four and a half mile length made it the longest water bridge in the world. Originally built as a privately owned toll bridge, the bridge was later bought by the State of Virginia after the endeavor went bankrupt. The original two lane bridge was replaced in 1982 with a four lane divided bridge with a center lift structure that provides 60 feet of vertical clearance when closed and 145 feet when opened. Our own boats require 50 feet of vertical clearance, but as we approached the span, the foreshortening visual effect when looking up made it appear almost certain that we would collide with the superstructure of the bridge. We collectively held our breaths as we slid below the span.

James River "Ghost Fleet"

Once past the bridge, the helm was turned over to Karl who enjoyed his first efforts at sailing *Second Wind*. On a broad reach, he drove us northwest and then north past Fort Crawford and into the "ghost fleet." This portion of the National Defense Reserve Fleet, called the "James River Fleet" or the "Ghost Fleet," is a "mothballed" collection of merchant vessels. Many of the ships are old deactivated hulls that are decaying and waiting to be scrapped. Some of the better ships could be activated within 20 to 120 days to provide shipping for the United States. The fleet is managed by the U.S. Department of Transportation's Maritime Administration (MARAD). The Merchant Ship Sales Act of 1946 established a National Defense Reserve Fleet to serve as a reserve of ships for national defense and national emergencies. Vessels from this fleet have served in seven wars and crises, including the Korean War where 540 vessels were commissioned to move military forces. During a worldwide shortfall of ships in 1951–53, more than 600 ships were reactivated to carry coal to northern Europe and grain to India. From 1955 through

1964, another 600 ships were used to store grain for the Department of Agriculture. Another 223 cargo ships and 29 tankers were activated during a tonnage shortfall after the Suez Canal was closed in 1956. During the Berlin crisis of 1961, 18 vessels were activated and remained in service until 1970. Another 172 vessels were activated for the Vietnam War. The James River Fleet of ships are rafted and anchored in the channel off Ft. Eustis where the James bends north at Mulberry Island. The ships are today unmanned and electronically monitored.

Carter's Grove Plantation

We passed the fleet and continued northwest where at red buoy "32" we sighted "Carter's Grove" Plantation off the starboard bow. This plantation home stands as another reminder of the great wealth amassed behind tobacco farming in the tidewaters of the Chesapeake during the colonial period. The plantation home was built in 1755 on the north bank of the James River by Carter Burwell, the grandson of Robert "King" Carter. King Carter was one of the wealthiest and most influential men in mid 18th century Virginia. The home represents one of the finest Georgian Plantation style homes built in the colonies and is noted for its brickwork and rich interior finishes. The house remained essentially unaltered until 1928, when the property was modernized and enlarged. The roof was heightened to accommodate a third floor, dormers were added, and the dependencies were enlarged and connected to the main house with hyphens.

In 1969, the Colonial Williamsburg Foundation acquired the property and opened the house as a museum, along with reconstructed slave quarters to present both sides of plantation life. The extensive garden was reconstructed after detailed archeological investigations. Those excavations also uncovered the site of Wolstenholme Town, an early 17th century settlement founded by investors of the London Company of Virginia. The Colonial Williamsburg Foundation sold Carter's Grove to a private citizen in December 2007, closing the plantation to the public.

Aerial View of Kings Mill Marina

At 4:00 in the afternoon, against a strong current pushing down stream, we turned north at the red "40" buoy and headed into King's Mill Marina. Once docked, the crew quickly headed to the deck of the James Landing Grille which overlooked the marina. With temperatures in the mid 90's, air conditioning and cold drinks were in significant demand. Christer and Steve remained behind to work on an air conditioning system that continued to defy their best engineering attempts to repair it. Their final assessment was that it lacked refrigerant. But with strict environmental controls over servicing refrigerants in air conditioners, they were unable to find a registered service technician to refill the unit.

Kings Mill proved to be a hidden surprise, and by Tuesday morning its pleasures had led to open mutiny. As boats were being prepared for sea, the women crew members, who had tolerated heat and discomfort long enough, abandoned ship for the restaurant deck and drinks. A short while later, the skippers were informed that an official mutiny had been declared. The crew decided that the pool, fitness center, and dining options at the resort were of more interest than another hot day at sea. We were staying a second night. With temperatures again in the low 90's, the women headed for the pool as the men negotiated an extended stay with an accommodating marina staff who could not have been more understanding.

Second Wind at Kings Mill Waiting for the Tide

Destination: Chickahominy River
Wednesday, June 26, 2013
(12.3 Nautical Miles, 3 Hours)

Second Wind Aground

On Wednesday morning, after a day of leisure and recreation, we assembled a reluctant crew and tried to depart the marina. However, as we tried to pull clear of our slip we discovered that *Second Wind* was solidly aground at the dock. We struggled to free ourselves of the mud by hoisting sail and trying to drive the boat off of a few inches of bottom. But our efforts proved fruitless, and we waited out the tide to lift us free. By ten we were again headed up the James.

At noon we stood off Jamestown Island, the site of England's first successful settlement on North America's mainland. The site is today memorialized by the Jamestown National Historic Monument and "The Jamestown Settlement", a living history interpretive site. These are operated by the Jamestown Yorktown Foundation in conjunction with the Commonwealth of Virginia.

Jamestown Settlement

Rothrock wrote extensively of his visit to Jamestown. He noted that during his visit, *"Even the ruins of Jamestown have almost disappeared. Fragments of the old magazine remain, and also a portion of the church tower; but these, with the cemetery back of the church, are the only visible memorials of a time and a settlement which we regret have left so few monuments. It is evident, however, from the scattered bricks and the faint indications of old cellars and the like, that the settlement covered a considerable area."*

Today, no original structure remains from the first colony except for the archeological digs on the island. These extensive archaeological investigations have been ongoing since 1994 and have uncovered many discoveries including hundreds of thousands of artifacts, a large portion of them from the first few years of the settlement's history. Two months before our voyage, the Smithsonian's National Museum of Natural History and archaeologists from Jamestown announced the discovery of the bones of a 14-year-old girl discovered in these digs. There were clear signs that she was cannibalized. The human remains date back to the deadly winter of 1609-1610, known as the "starving time" in Jamestown, when hundreds of colonists died.

Founded in 1607, Jamestown would remain the seat of colonial Virginia government until 1699 when Williamsburg assumed the central place of governance around which English development would center.

The first English colonists arrived in Virginia on May 14, 1607, and selected this small island for their new settlement. The Virginia Company, who sponsored the colonization, advised the selection of a settlement location that could be easily defended from European states colonizing and trading in the new world, notably the Dutch, French, and Spanish. The island met this condition, providing an effective view up and down the James River. The island was also far enough upriver to minimize contact with ships from hostile nations as they traded and traversed the Chesapeake Bay. The river adjacent to the island was deep enough to anchor ships and support trade. The site was not previously occupied by the American Indians because it was swampy, prone to flooding, and located away from good hunting grounds. The colonists were ill prepared for the new world, and relied significantly on English resupply ships and Indian trade to survive. The poor swampy land, a drought, ill preparation in farming crops, and conflicts in leadership took a terrible toll on the colony. During the winter of 1609-1610 most of the colony would die off with only 60 out of 214 colonists surviving. By June 1610 the colonists were actively abandoning the settlement when supply ships carrying a new Governor arrived. This event allowed the desperate colony to survive on marginal life support. By 1611, a majority of the colonists who had arrived at the Jamestown settlement had died. The colony was failing economically with very few exports shipped to England. Only financial incentives, including a promise from King James I to new investors of more land to the west, kept the colony from collapse. It wasn't until 1618 when tobacco was established as an export crop that the investment and growth of the Virginia colony was able to flourish. But the crop required labor, and so the expanding plantation community in the new world turned to bondsmen and slaves to build new wealth. The expansion of tobacco exports and slavery went hand in hand, and both have as their source this small island on the James. It should be remembered that tobacco gave rise to two great cancers in America, the cancer of slavery and the body cancer from cigarettes. The human pain and suffering from both has been immeasurable.

Rothrock noted during his visit to Jamestown, *"The most interesting ruin of Old Jamestown is, of course, its church tower. One marvels that a church so large as this was (judging from the ruined tower) could have been erected at so early a period in colonial history. It is to be remembered that to the men of those times (at least, to the better part of them) worship was something more than a luxury. I did not measure the tower (as I should have done), but should say it had a square base of about twenty feet. The remains still rise say twenty-five feet, and are entered by a fine large doorway. The bricks, of course, were brought from England. The first question which naturally suggests itself is: Why should a spot so full of sacred and patriotic memories as this is be allowed to fall into ruin, and to be overgrown by weeds? Or, worse still, why should it be allowed to remain so? Alas for mankind! The proprietor apologized for the appearance of the ground, and said, "I would gladly open it up and uncover the graves, were it not for the fact that to do so would simply be to make them more accessible to curiosity-seekers. Men come to the old tower and carry off the young ivy shoots; they break the tombstones, and nothing is so sacred as to prevent its destruction." From what I saw, there could be no doubt about the truth of his statement.*

Through the gateway of the tower we passed into the old graveyard, over what was probably the site of the body of the church. Here and there an opening in the rank underbrush and weeds revealed a tombstone or sepulchral slab, and on some of these an inscription may be made out. Time has dealt harshly with the lettering, and in some cases almost destroyed the characters. There is a remarkable instance of the effect of tree growth, furnished by a buttonwood tree (Platanus occidentalis) which stood by the side of a grave. Since the time of burial this has grown into a very large tree. Meanwhile its lateral growth encroached upon the horizontal slab covering the grave, and also carried it upward slightly. Hence the stone became imbedded in the base of the tree, and was also subjected to a considerable vertical strain. The two forces fractured it. Mr. Brown informs me that human agency aided in its further destruction afterward. There was no date to indicate the age of the grave.

From other graves I copied the following inscriptions :

"Under this Stone lies interred

The Body of

Mrs. Hannah Ludwell,

Relict of

The Hon. Philip Ludwell, Esq.,

By whom She has left

One Son and Two Daughters.

After a most exemplary Life,

Spent in chearful Innocence

And exercise of

Piety, Charity, and Hospitality,

She Patiently submitted to

Death on the 4th Day of April, 1731, in the 52

Year of Her Age."

Another reads :

> *"Here Lyeth William Sherwood,*
> *That Was Born in the Parish*
> *of White Chappel Near*
> *London. A great Sinner*
> *Waiting for a Joyfull*
> *Resurrection."*

Twin Rivers Yacht Club

At 1:00 in the afternoon we arrived at the mouth of the Chickahominy River where today the Twin Rivers Yacht Club, a man made marina excavated along the shore, serves as a private yacht club located in a country club community. The harbor master could not have been more accommodating to a hot crew, and brought down a golf cart to shuttle us up to the clubhouse for a late lunch. With afternoon thunderstorms threatening, and temperatures in the 90's, the crew decided to remain in the air conditioned clubhouse after lunch. The skippers headed back early to do some maintenance on the boats and to again work on the broken air conditioning system. The storms trapped the crew at the club until late evening. The storms did pass eventually, and the crew returned to a quiet, muggy night onboard the boats.

Twin Rivers Beach On The James

Rothrock was to reach the mouth of the Chickahominy on the evening of June 22nd. He would write of the land where the yacht club now stands, "… *we anchored south of the Chickahominy, and next morning ran over to photograph the mouth of this historic river. In itself it is nothing but a good-sized stream, opening through swamps and low, pine-covered bluffs into the James. For all this, however, it has been the scene of some of the most important events witnessed in our short colonial and federal life. Captain John Smith, very soon after the location of the settlers upon Jamestown Island, set out to explore the Chickahominy region, which, though nominally under control of Powhatan, was directly governed by his brother Opechancanough, who from first to last was hostile to the whites. It was on this trip that Smith was captured, and marched from village to village by his captors, then doomed to execution, and rescued from the jaws of death by Pocahontas...*

Still more history has been made for Virginia along the banks of the Chickahominy. In 1616, owing to the almost exclusive attention which was paid by the colonists to the culture of tobacco, there was not enough of corn for food. The Chickahominy Indians had promised a supply, but, seeing the straits to which the whites were reduced, refused contemptuously to deliver the stipulated quantity. This resulted in a fight, in which twelve Indians were killed and as many more captured. This for a time enforced peace; but only for a time. The Indians, a few years later, made a bloody retaliation, which threatened the very life of the young colony. The events of 1860 to 1864 along the famous little stream are still fresh in memory. At last white-winged Peace, in the shape of trading schooners, go up and down the Chickahominy giving Northern money in exchange for Virginia lumber. We may now well believe that its future will be as quiet as its past has been turbulent."

CHAPTER III
DOWN THE JAMES AND UP THE CHESAPEAKE

Destination: Newport News, VA
Thursday, June 27, 2013
(38.8 Nautical Miles, 6 Hours 30 Minutes)

With temperatures settling into the mid to upper 90's every day, the goal of repairing *CamiCat*'s air conditioner was now a high priority. The technical assessment of the equipment failure came down to low refrigerant, and a phone call to Bluewater Yachting Center in Hampton confirmed that they had a technician who could look at the system. Plans were made to leave Twin Rivers Yacht Club early on Thursday, and by 6:30 in the morning we were under sail with current and wind driving us down river. Lucia took her turn at the helm, and proved an able helmswoman, driving the boat to good speed.

By 7:30 we were approaching the Jamestown Ferry, a free automobile and bus ferry service across the James River at State Route 31. It connects Jamestown on the north bank of the James with Scotland Wharf on the south bank in Surry County. The ferry provides the only vehicle crossing of the river between the James River Bridge in Newport News and the Benjamin Harrison Memorial

Bridge upriver in Hopewell. It is operated 24 hours a day, 7 days a week by the Virginia Department of Transportation. The fifteen minute crossing is made by a two ferry system. And, as we passed, the ferries *Pocahontas* and *Williamsburg* made their crossings in front of us.

Scotland-Jamestown Ferry

Just beyond the north ferry landing we passed on our port side the replicas of Christopher Newport's three small ships, *Susan Constant*, *Godspeed*, and *Discovery*, which are docked at the Jamestown Settlement. The replicas are copies of the English Virginia Company's transport ships that brought the original settlers to Jamestown in the new world in 1606-1607. They are open to the public as tourist sites.

Replicas Of Christopher Newport's Three Ships

Continuing down river, we passed on the south shore, opposite Jamestown, Pleasant Point. This colonial plantation home was built in the late 1730s by William Edwards IV, whose family prospered in the 17th and 18th centuries through the tobacco industry. William was a tobacco inspector at nearby Gray's Creek. His home is a simple one and a half stories in elevation. It faces onto the river, with a terraced landscape down to the river at its front. The original patent to the Pleasant Point Plantation dates back to 1657 when the land was deeded to William Edwards, Gentleman. By 1700, the plantations owned by the Edwards family exceeded 6,200 acres, with tobacco as the primary crop.

Pleasant Point Plantation House

A short time later we were passing Hog Island to starboard. Rothrock would write about his journey past this bend in the James, *"Approaching the southern shore, just below Hog Island, as we were hunting a channel into a little creek, we found by the lead-line that for a long distance the bottom was almost absolutely flat. "One fathom" was the report, repeated until it became painfully monotonous. The lead indicated everywhere that soft mud was being evenly deposited. In many places an oar could be run down into it several feet with the utmost ease. The bluffs were once just as the river-bed now is, and, allowing sufficient time, the future student of geology may find the now-forming mud flats above the surface of the water, and point to them as being simply another page in the same natural history."*

These mud flats today sit off Surry Nuclear Power Plant where two nuclear reactors now provide 1.6 gigawatts of power for Dominion Power users in Virginia and North Carolina.

Rothrock continues, *"Passing Hog Island on our way down, we ran in along-shore, and spent Sunday at anchor near Ferguson's wharf, which is nearly abreast of the Point of Shoals light-house.*

The bluffs looked very inviting, and I expected to find something of interest there. We had seen a blue stratum exposed at several points along the river. Here it formed the base of the bluffs, and was very suggestive of tertiary deposits, which I had seen elsewhere. However, Lew anticipated me in the discovery. He soon returned to the yacht with the news that there was no end of such things (coral and fossil shells) on shore. I suggested that the coral might have come there as ballast from the West Indies; but Lew scouted the idea: "There is too much of it for that." So we went ashore together. The blue stratum was full of shells (pecten and its usual associates). Here and there the tide had undermined it, and masses fell to the tide-level, where the shells lay in profusion. The coral revealed itself just at the tide-line, and not in the bluff, but out in the water. So far as we could see, it was there as an immense mass, from which we broke off a fragment weighing about two hundred pounds. It never came there as ballast. As to its origin and its extent geologists may decide, if, indeed, they have not already done so long since. We that is, Lew and I, made considerable collections of these interesting things for the Philadelphia Academy of Natural Sciences."

Later, Rothrock's journey down stream into Hampton proved more difficult. He writes, *"June 25th gave us a strong head-wind, which, with the tide against us, made the run to Newport News a tedious one. No stop was made, as we had "done the place" on our way up the river."*

As the morning wore on, Lucia steered us past Cobham Bay, around Hogs Point, past the Ghost Fleet and Fort Crawford, back to Newport News and under the James River Bridge.

By 12:30 p.m. we were once again turning into Hampton Creek

and heading past Hampton University into Bluewater Yachting Center. Looking across the creek into the heart of Hampton University, we viewed a beautiful campus that Rothrock would be hard pressed to recognize as the one he visited in 1883. He wrote of this harbor that, *"We anchored on the evening of the 25th of June in Hampton Creek, among "oyster-pungies" and fishing-canoes. Negro life appears here, I may say, certainly in a most characteristic form; possibly, too, I may add, after considering all its obstacles, in a most promising form. Evidently very much of the old spirit the war of the races is still found in certain quarters in Hampton. "Nigger, light that lamp!" was the order given in a store of the village to a colored man of the establishment. The fact that it was silently obeyed would probably indicate that it was neither unusual nor unexpected. I will not add in which of the churches, I was afterward told that the white gentleman held a conspicuous place. However, time is a sovereign cure for many diseases. Probably in another generation such specimens of linguistic pathology will be studied even there with about the same interest and disgust as that with which a microscopist of to-day examines a section from any other festering sore."*

Hampton University

There is no doubt that Rothrock would be delighted by the success of Hampton University and its progress since his visit. In his reflections on the school 130 years ago he writes, *"Less obtrusive by far than the stirring events of the past, what is now being done toward educating the Indian and the colored races must leave a trail of light in the future. It will yet be reckoned among the first clear, shining acts of justice toward those with whom our dealings in the past have been dark as infamy. If we credit the Hampton School with no higher results than those of an experiment, thus far successful, we cannot over-estimate the importance of what it has accomplished. What is to be done with the Indians? Probably Hampton and other like schools will soon teach us.*

Its great mission is with the Negro. A curse follows a crime closely; and the curse is looming up dark and threatening. If slavery was once fitly characterized as the black plague, what shall we say of the ignorance it engendered among those who were the victims? Emancipation, irrespective of its righteousness, became a war measure necessary for the salvation of the country. With it came the right of suffrage, as naturally as sunshine comes with the sun. But a vote is a vote, whether cast by an intellectual giant or by a mental dwarf, and has as much weight in one case as in the other. In this is the well-recognized danger; for the perpetuity of republican government is assured only as long as the majority is intelligent as well as honest. Couple these evident truths with the fact that the rate of increase is vastly greater among the uneducated black race than among the more cultured whites. This is the whole truth and the whole danger, and this, then, the curse: that those whom we once enslaved and degraded threaten to subvert even the power that at last invested them with the dignity of a full citizenship. Shall the vigorous free black, with his enormous rate of multiplication, sometimes vengeful, usually injudicious, come to doom finally the very institutions which, as a slave, he has already so greatly endangered?

Hampton School demands not only national aid in its projected work, but national gratitude as well. Every educated colored man it sends forth is a pledge to the future. Considering the difficulties which lay in the road of the institution, it is no longer an experiment, but an astounding success.

Copying from the official report of the school, which bears date of June 30, 1882, I find the following statements of Mrs. E. C. Dixon: "Of the 389 graduates and 37 Senior undergraduates those who left before the end of the third year entered in the new ' Record-Book :' (males, 280; females, 146; total, 426), I have learned that 326 have engaged in teaching, and that more than three-fourths of the whole i.e., 319 have made teaching their vocation since they left the institute; three are licensed preachers, as well as teachers. Over ninety percent have engaged in teaching. Of the whole number 27 have died; 2 became insane; leaving 397 to be ' kept track of.' .... One can hardly help noticing the overwhelming proportion of those students who went South, where they could render the most signal service. Such a showing leads inevitably to the conclusion, that, together with the knowledge imparted, the institute must keep constantly before its students what is their manifest destiny and their highest moral obligation.

We owe support to a school that does so much toward removing the national danger from ignorance, and substitutes for it, hope and high possibilities.

Besides the mere matter of education, in its common acceptation, we must also remember the trades which the negro has a chance of learning there, some of which, at least, he can learn in very few other places. Hence the tendency of the work done in the school is not only to place the pupil on a respectable plane of life, but to enable him to hold his position in future. The full import of this can be understood only when it is remembered that over a large portion of the United States there are trades' unions from which the negro is systematically excluded, and by which, so far as may be, he is prevented from acquiring a trade. I am simply mentioning the fact, not criticizing it. In truth, bad as the principle may be, it is in reality no worse than Wall Street gambling in the property of others, or than a wheat corner in Chicago, which speculates in the daily bread of the laboring man. Neither of these is worse than the others, for all spring from the law of self-protection first, and then grow into inordinate selfishness at last.

How well the Hampton work is done appears from the following extract, taken from the memorandum - sheet accompanying the "Report for 1882 :"Our printing-office, book-bindery, harness-, tin-, wood-working, and shoe-shops, will gladly compete for work wholly on the merit and the prices of the articles made."[Signed, S. C. Armstrong, principal.]

Two large farms and a saw-mill, besides the above-named industries, give to the willing and energetic students further means of supporting themselves while receiving their education.

In a volume like the present it would be out of place to go more into detail than we have.

The Indians, of whom there were ninety-two in attendance during the year ending June, 1882, appear to be mainly, or in part, at least, supported by the government, that is, the United States government pays one hundred and sixty-seven dollars apiece for each of one hundred Indian lads. This does not include, or meet the expense of tuition, which costs, besides, about seventy dollars a year for each student.

From the report of Miss Isabel B. Eustis, I quote the following pithy passages: "The success of the education of our Indians turns upon the conditions which await them on their return to their homes. We believe in their ability to stand in an ordinarily healthful moral atmosphere. The false conditions of life which exist in an Indian agency, the difficulty of obtaining healthful sympathy or wise restraint make their task of stemming the current of savage life an almost superhuman one. The girls have no foot-hold on which to attempt to breast it. The boys have their trades, and can separate themselves from their old homes and their camp life. There is absolutely no position of dignity to which an Indian girl can look forward after three years of training, with any reasonable confidence. There is nothing for her but to enjoy or suffer the present as best she may."..."Should the United States government ever find it possible to keep their treaty with the Sioux tribe, which provides for a school and suitable teacher for every thirty children in the tribe, the way might open for the solution of the knotty problem. "Such schools located among all the Indian tribes "would give honorable work, full of inspiration to our best Indian girls. " Just one extract more to show the other side, the absence of such suitable employment. This I take from the report of Lieut. George Leroy Brown : "The girls must be prepared to stand up against a ' sea of trouble' and temptation.

There is one more aspect to this question of practical philanthropy which is working out a solution of so many social and political problems and dangers. Those who lead in such movements are, in a large number of instances, ladies, women of character, culture, and refinement, who endure the work and the sacrifices connected with it from the very best and purest principles. Yet to these very pioneers our leading colleges, in most instances, deny the advantages of an education which would be cheerfully accorded to the pupils of those ladies. It is useless to decry this as an act of flagrant injustice; just now our eyes are blinded when we look at the question. But some sort of moral revolution will come, nay, is coming, by which the scales will be removed; and we will then ask, how could we ever have been party to such a wrong?

It is right that the Negro or the Indian should be admitted to the best college course, when prepared for it. But how can it be right that his teacher shall be deprived of like advantages?

Do the ordinary avocations of daily life, where the sexes mingle without restraints, justify the fears of our conservative college rulers? The day is probably not far distant when public institutions, instead of being judged by what they think of themselves, may be measured by their aggressive power for the widest usefulness; and when neither age, respectability of teaching force, well-equipped laboratories, nor crowded library shelves will atone for the sin of narrowness."

Hampton University

Hampton University today has an enrollment of 5,400 students, with a course of studies that includes: Liberal Arts, Business, Science, Engineering & Technology, Education, Nursing, Pharmacy, and Journalism. Founded in 1868 as the Hampton Normal and Agricultural Institute, the academic program evolved over the years from a secondary school to a four-year college, and then into a university. With this growth the school's name changed to Hampton Institute in 1930, and then to Hampton University in 1984. Starting with the purchase of a small farm known as "Little Scotland," the school was founded with a purpose " to train selected Negro youth who should go out and teach and lead their people first by example, by getting land and homes; to give them not a dollar that they could earn for themselves; to teach respect for labor, to replace stupid drudgery with skilled hands, and in this way to build up an industrial system for the sake not only of self-support and intelligent labor, but also for the sake of character."

In 1872 Booker T. Washington enrolled in the institute, becoming the most distinguished of the school's many accomplished graduates. Washington was born into slavery to Jane, an enslaved woman, and a white plantation father. Emancipation brought Washington freedom at the age of 9, and with freedom his family moved to West Virginia where his mother was reunited with her husband. Washington worked in a variety of manual labor jobs in West Virginia before making his way to Hampton Roads seeking an education. He worked his way through Hampton Normal and Agricultural Institute and attended college at Wayland Seminary, now Virginia Union University. After returning to Hampton as a teacher, he was named, in 1881, as the first leader of the new Tuskegee Institute in Alabama. He went on to national fame for his advocacy of African-American education. Washington played a dominant role in black politics, winning wide support in the black community and among progressive whites in the North. He gained access to top national leaders in politics, philanthropy and education in his quest to establish and operate thousands of small community schools and institutions of higher education for the betterment of blacks throughout the South.

Once we were docked, the afternoon heat set in with a terrible fury. The crews headed to the marina restaurant while Christer and Steve went in search of an air conditioning technician. By 2:00 in the afternoon it was clear that the air conditioning technician was not to be found, and Christer and Steve were implementing "Plan B" which was to buy a window air conditioning unit and mount it in the cabin-way hatch. While this effort unfolded, Karl and Lucia were to retrieve their car from Fort Monroe and close out their part of the adventure by departing north by way of the Chesapeake Bay Bridge Tunnel. Better company could not have been found, and Karl left with a bet over who was to be the first grandfather between us.

With the new air conditioner running at full blast, Christer and Camilla hosted supper in their now frigid cabin. And, as the evening wore on and bottles of wine were enjoyed, Christer finally pulled out the "Pig Game". This game is a Finnish game of chance where plastic pigs are rolled and points awarded for the various ways in which the pigs might land. Although we never really understood the rules, we did enjoy the shouts and laughs as pigs landed in various contortions, and even as the wine disappeared, the variations of pigs landing in even more contorted ways generated wild laughter. At night's end, Cece and I discovered to our surprise that we had won the game without ever really understanding how.

Destination: Piankatank River, VA
Friday, June 28, 2013
(24.6 Nautical Miles, 4 Hours 45 Minutes)

Early Friday morning, Steve and Dee left *CamiCat* and headed back to their home in North Carolina. After refueling, *Second Wind* and *CamiCat* cast off from Hampton's docks and headed east towards the Chesapeake. As we ran past Fort Wool we passed two massive warships returning to port. One was the *USS Wasp* a multipurpose amphibious assault ship. She is the tenth U.S. Navy vessel to bear the name *Wasp*, and she is the lead ship of her class. She was built specifically to accommodate new air cushioned landing craft for fast troop movement over the beach. She also supports Harrier II vertical/short take-off and landing jets. At 843 feet in length and with a 105 foot beam, she dwarfed the channel as we passed her on our starboard side.

USS Wasp Returning to Port

With southwest winds, we ran along Buckroe Beach and then past the mouth of the York River on a broad reach. By mid day we were off New Point Comfort Light watching thunderstorms beginning to form to the west. Checking our charts and weather radar, we realized that we would not outrun the storms before reaching Antipoison Creek, our planned destination for the day, so we looked again to the Piankatank as a river of refuge. As we set course around Gwynn Island and into the Piankatank we watched massive storm clouds begin to move to the northwest. With strong winds building from the southwest we found Fishing Bay too rough to anchor, and so turned back to Godfrey Bay which was better protected from the approaching storms. Once the anchors were set, the winds built precipitously and we sat back in our cockpits and watched lightning flash across the sky to our north. We never felt the full effects of the storm as it did pass north, but we witnessed along the storm's edge one of those remarkable displays of nature as the sky lit up and thunder roared.

Summer Thunderstorm Passing North

On the bluff along the western shore of Godfrey Bay at its mouth, we sited the Georgian plantation home "Hesse". This tobacco plantation was built by the Armistead family after 500 acres of land were patented to Henry Armistead in 1659. By the time the property was sold out of the family, after the Revolution, the plantation had grown to 3,900 acres. "Hesse" is another historic reminder of the period along the Chesapeake when economic prosperity was driven by tobacco production and slave labor under colonial rule. The plantation home sits about one hundred yards from shore and stands as a five bay, two-story home sixty feet long and thirty two feet deep. The five bay flanking wing was built in 1952 and is not part of the original colonial era plantation home.

"Hesse" Plantation House

As the storm passed, we treated Christer and Camilla to a very pleasant evening onboard *Second Wind* and to a supper of taco salad and cold beer.

Rothrock's voyage north was into Antipoison Creek, and he captured his day's sail this way, *"Wind and weather often interfere with the plans of yachtsmen. My own experience did not in this respect differ from that of those who sailed before me. So with this explanation I must leave the large remainder of interesting facts concerning this most noteworthy region untold. What Fortress Monroe now is need not be stated, for others have done so more fully than I can do.*

A delightful, easy southerly wind carried us up the shore, past Back River, which was once the scene of General Magruder's military operations. The ground is now devoted to labors more peaceful, more odorous, and more useful. An establishment for the extraction of oil from the small fish known as "moss-bunker" stands in sight from the bay. These fish swim in schools, and may be recognized by the dark color they give the surface water. The refuse remainder, left after extracting the oil, is ground up and forms the basis of a fertilizer which is in considerable demand by agriculturists. That the business is lucrative may be supposed from the vast number of vessels engaged in the capture of these fish. Almost every inlet of considerable size along-shore has one or more "fish-mills," where "the catch" is "worked up." How long the industry will last at the present rate of destruction of the fish is a problem which we cannot yet solve. Those engaged in the business did not mention to me any scarcity of fish. Indeed, at Newport News the James River appeared to be dotted over with the dark schools. Between catching oysters in winter and the fish in summer, these amphibious beings, negroes and poor whites, manage to eke out a living, such as it is. The negro workers I saw at one fish-mill, which shall be nameless, were as degraded a looking lot of human beings as I ever met. But for the fact of their speaking English one might have supposed they were fresh from the "Guinea Coast."

It is a puzzle to me to understand how a man can labor amid the filth, the stench, and the associations of such an establishment, and still retain anything of purity, though I know some men who do; nevertheless, I cannot understand it.

As noon of the 28th of June approached, we rounded Too's Point light-house, on the York River, and looked long and eagerly before we saw Yorktown. A mere glance at the bluffs, which front the river, would leave on the mind of an observer the impression that these and the ground back of them were an ideal battle-field. There is very little concerning the place that remains unsaid. If I were obliged to offer an opinion at all concerning the town, I should say that neither fire nor war could damage its appearance very much. Time was when I regarded the surrender of Cornwallis as due entirely to the courage of our troops. I am now inclined to think he wanted to get away from the place badly enough to make almost any reasonable sacrifice. I have no doubt he would have left earlier had he found it possible to do so.

The evening of June 28th found us anchored in Antepoisen Creek, that is, in the hook made by the northern shore, which is guarded by Rappahannock Spit light-house. What evil genius inspired those who named Mob-Jack Bay, Stingray Point, Antepoisen Creek? Our run had been only about thirty-five miles. The wind was fair, though most of the way very light. So far as I am able to say, I think that, during the month of June, morning and evening can generally be depended upon for a breeze from some quarter in Chesapeake Bay. There is almost as certainly a trying noon calm, during which the sun beats down with a most intense fervor. Squalls, to be dreaded, often come during June and July, and their usual time of appearance is towards evening. Our harbor in Antepoisen Creek was another of the many beautiful ones, such as we had hitherto found. Near its head we were completely landlocked and had about two fathoms of water under the bow, just such a place as one can sleep most soundly in. There was no fear of anything."

Destination: Great Wicomico River, VA
Saturday, June 29, 2013
(43.1 Nautical Miles, 7 Hours 30 Minutes)

Saturday had us up early to try to capture aerial photos of Godfrey Bay and the "Hesse" Plantation. Photographs were taken from the mast head with a camera sling Christer had crafted and hoisted aloft. After a slow turn around Godfrey Bay for pictures, we headed down the Piankatank and motored again out into the Chesapeake.

Second Wind Headed Up the Bay

Heading up the Bay, once again on a broad reach with winds from the southwest, we passed the mouth of the Rappahannock River and then Antipoison Creek, where Rothrock had anchored 130 years before us. Continuing north, we reached the mouth of the Great Wicomico River just after noon, and then turned west into Ingram

Bay. Once past the red number "6" buoy, we turned north into Cockrell Creek and steered towards the town of Reedville.

The Menhaden Fleet of Reedville

Cockrell Creek is home to the Atlantic menhaden fishing industry. We passed numerous industrial fishing boats tied up on both the eastern and western shores of the creek. Once among the fishing craft, we were overcome by the horrific smell of fish processing. A small oily fish, menhaden are found in great abundance in the Bay. The processing of the fish into oil is a steam process whose byproduct is one of the most pungent odors imaginable. The smell followed us into Reedville as we traveled upstream. We soon tried to escape the smell by docking at the Crazy Crab Restaurant, and sought the protection of indoor airconditioning. After a late lunch, we walked up through historic Reedville to the Fisherman's museum.

Historic Reedville Waterfront

The history of Reedville is linked to the commercial fishing industry that developed here in the late 19th century. In 1874, nine years before Rothrock's cruise, Elijah Reed moved his menhaden fishing operation from Brooklin, Maine, to Cockrell's Creek. The industry flourished, especially in the early part of the 20th century. Today, Reedville is one of the largest ports in the United States for the landing of commercial fish, second only to Kodiak, Alaska. The museum does a wonderful job of telling the history of the fishing fleets and their technology. They also have on display the skipjack *Claud W. Somers* and the deck boat *Elva C.*, both entered into the National Register of Historic Places. Wealthy factory owners and boat captains built magnificent homes along Reedville's main street and our walk back to the boats was a wonderful look back at Victorian, Queen Anne, Colonial Revival and Greek Revival architectural styles. After finding the local ice cream parlor, we made our way back to the boats and headed up Back Creek to drop anchor and spend the night.

Rothrock's trip into the Great Wicomico took place on June 30th

1883 of which he wrote *"… we started early, hoping to make the harbor in the mouth of the Patuxent. This was only about forty-five miles in a direct line. Knowing the uncertainty of the wind, we desired to take every advantage that time could give us; hence an unusually early start. At first we had a fair wind, and plenty of it; it was right "astern" also. Before we reached the Great Wicomico it was "dead ahead," and when we fairly opened the mouth of the Potomac there was a calm. This at first was simply an annoyance. We supposed it was merely one of the lulls we had so often experienced before, and endeavored to comfort ourselves by such philosophy. Hour after hour passed, but no wind came. The tide was carrying us down and across the bay, just the direction we did not want to go. Then annoyance deepened into exasperation (senseless, to be sure), as the little yacht was tossed like a feather on the heavy swell. There was not a trace of air. Never before did I so fully realize what was meant by a dead calm. With each lurch of the boat the blocks creaked and the sails flapped heavily from side to side. The heat was more than the word intense implies; it was scorching, and the glare from the superheated deck was almost unendurable. What was the pleasure in yachting? None, under such circumstances. So that entire day passed. Exasperation gave place to, well, call it fear. "All men are cowards at times," and it only renders matters worse to add to the weakness of fear the sin of prevarication.*

All day the barometer had been going down. It was certain that a storm was impending. East, south, and west were filled with heavy clouds. We could hear the heavy thunder, and see the vivid lightning flash across the sky. Would there be enough of wind before the squall burst upon us to enable us to make some harbor? Or must we too stand the onset in our little boat out in the middle of the bay? These questions were never uttered, though I am quite sure they were inwardly asked by both Lew and myself.

Later in the afternoon a slight wind was seen coming over the water towards us from the mouth of the Potomac. It came so slowly that we feared it would die away before reaching us. After what appeared like an age it began to be felt, first fanning our cheeks, then filling our sails; and in a few minutes more we were quietly slipping through the water, back toward Great Wicomico, which we had passed early in the morning. This, to be sure, was not where we wanted to go, but choice was lost in thankfulness to reach any harbor. In two hours, just as darkness had fairly settled around us, we let our anchor go in a quiet arm of the Great Wicomico. It was a lovely, secluded little bay, in full sight of one of the greatest fishing establishments of the Chesapeake, a perfect, "restful" place that we had found for the morrow, which was the Sabbath.

During the night the storm came; and, as we heard the wind whistling fiercely through the rigging, and felt the yach't rocking on the waves, we thought even kindly of the breeze which had carried us away from our destination, but into perfect safety.

I have related the experience of that day to show the most dismal side of yachting by sail. If one has a long purse and no end of generosity, if he is willing to keep a floating home for sailors, to be simply a passenger on his own boat, to go when and where his sailing-master directs, then a large steam-yacht is much better. I was yachting under other circumstances and with other objects in view; and, furthermore, as the season wore along, I gradually came to prefer risking my boat under my own directions than to accept what greater skill the presence of a sailing-master might bring. I will simply add : yacht-owner, learn the rudiments, go slowly, but command your own craft. If there be any manhood in the sport, that will bring it out. If there is not, then it were better abandoned.

I must, however, say this: if one can find another Lew, then he is fortunate. Lew is equal to any emergency likely to occur on a small craft. Entering the harbor I have described, our boat, though drawing only a little over two feet of water, grounded. While I was off in the yawl boat hunting the channel he jumped overboard and pushed the yacht into deep water. By the time she was fairly floating I had found the channel, and we were soon in our Sunday harbor."

Destination: Solomon's Island, MD
Sunday, June 30, 2013
(44.3 Nautical Miles, 10 Hours)

Sunday morning both crews woke early, as the wind had shifted and driven the worst of the fish processing smells through the portals of the boats. There was no escaping the smell in our bunks, and so by 7:00 we had departed. Light rain was falling as we motored out of Cockrell Creek into the Great Wicomico and finally into the Bay. Quartering seas tossed the *Second Wind* until we were able to turn north and run with the wind. Surfing off the waves, we progressed up the Bay to Smith Point Light Station and across the mouth of the Potomac into Maryland. Off No Point Light we passed the *Sicsbee*, a skipjack sailing south under mainsail. *Sicsbee* was built in 1901 at Deal Island, Maryland. She is one of the 35 surviving Chesapeake Bay skipjacks, and a member of the last commercial sailing fleet in the United States located at Tilghman, MD. At 47 feet long and with a 15 ½ feet beam, she draws only 3 feet 10 inches.

The skipjack arose near the end of the 19th century as an oyster dredging boat. Dredging was made legal in 1865, but boats of the time were unsuitable for the shallow water oyster harvesting. The predominant Chesapeake bugeye design of the time was adapted to a shallower design in order to provide a boat with more power that could work the shallow waters of the oyster beds.

The bugeye that Rothrock noted on his cruise was originally constructed with a log hull. But, as the supply of appropriate timber was exhausted and construction costs rose, builders looked to new hull designs. They adapted the sharpies of Long Island Sound by increasing the beam and simplifying the sail plan. The result was cheaper and simpler to construct than the bugeye, and it quickly became the predominant oyster work boat on the Bay.

Skipjack *Sicsbee* Under Sail

Maryland's oyster harvests reached an all-time peak in 1884, just one years after Rothrock's cruise. That year's harvest was approximately 15 million bushels of oysters. The oyster harvest has since declined steadily, especially at the end of the 20th century. The reported harvest during the 2011-12 season of 137,000 bushels is less than one percent of its 1884 peak. Maryland once had an estimated 200,000 acres of oyster reefs. Today, it has less than 36,000 acres. Pre-colonial oyster populations could have filtered the Bay's waters in less than four days. By 1988, the depletion of the oyster population had increased this filtration period to 325 days. A combination of factors has led to the oyster collapse, including pollution, human overpopulation, overfishing, and disease. Bay oysters are now close to extinction.

Gennaker Sheet Wrapped Around *CamiCat's* Propeller

Shortly after passing the *Sicsbee* we received a call from *CamiCat* in need of assistance. While running before the wind, with her asymmetrical gennaker flying, she had a sheet wrap around her freewheeling propeller. Movement through the water resulted in the sheet pounding the hull, and Christer was concerned the whipping line would compromise her fiberglass hull. Christer decided to dive under the boat to try to free the line from the propeller. In three foot seas, off Point No Point, we hailed a second boat passing by and both boats stood by as Christer went over the side. *CamiCat* rolled in the high seas as Christer fought to free the propeller and line. Close to exhaustion, Christer eventually returned onboard with the bitter end of the sheet, but with the line still wrapping the propeller. With only one engine operating on *CamiCat*, the boats returned to their course as the winds rose and a storm started building over the Patuxent River.

As we pulled into the Patuxent, we watched a massive updraft build over the southern shore of the river, and a storm moved over the Solomons with heavy downpours. Standing offshore, we watched the storm form and updrafts spin into what appeared to be strong circulating motion. The rains and winds appeared to verge on becoming a tornado, and caution kept us standing off. Eventually, at about 4:30, the storm passed and we ran into Zahniser's Yachting Center on Back Creek. Shore side assistance helped get *CamiCat* in under one engine.

Rotating Updraft Forming At Storm Center

By 6:00 that evening, Patrick, Dan and John joined the *Second Wind* for the final six days of the voyage, and Cece left to return to the grind of work. The Dry Dock Restaurant was our retreat for dinner. Half way through the meal, we got the call from my son Justin and daughter-in-law Hanny to report that they were at the hospital in labor, with expectations that a baby would soon be greeting the world.

At 1:00 in the morning on Monday July 1st, Justin called with the news that I was a grandfather, and a seven pound eleven ounce healthy girl was in the arms of her mother. It was difficult falling back asleep, and a quick phone call to Cece confirmed that she had also gotten the news. My memory transported me back thirty one years, when I held Justin in my arms for the first time. With each new life there comes so much promise and hope for the future.

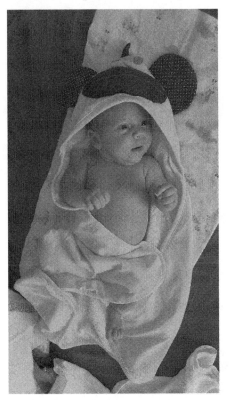

Olivia Welcomes a New World

Monday morning dawned with rain and threats of bad weather, so the decision was made to explore Solomon's Island rather than fight a stormy Bay crossing. In the late 1600's, the island was called Bourne's Island, and later Somervell's Island during the colonial era. Solomon's Island takes its name from 19th century Baltimore businessman Isaac Solomon who built a cannery on the island shortly after the Civil War. On the island, Solomon's house still stands.

Aerial Photo of Zahniser's Yachting Center

After some boat repairs and a trip to a local ship's store, the crew set off to the Calvert Marine Museum. The museum is dedicated to the collection, preservation, research, and interpretation of the culture and natural history of Southern Maryland. The museum's displays are directed to three themes: regional paleontology, estuarine life, and maritime history of these waters. A collection of exhibits, a marsh walk, the Drum Point Lighthouse, and a small craft collection provided us a very rewarding afternoon. It also offered us much greater insight into the Bay's development, its watercraft and culture. At closing we headed back to the boats where Patrick was preparing a culinary feast of pork and potatoes for supper.

Rothrock's sail into Solomon's Island was made on Monday, July 2, 1883, of which he wrote, " ... *we were off, and with a stiff breeze astern soon passed the mouth of the Potomac. I do not know whether, or not, this river is usually treacherous, but it has so happened, that both my friends, with whom I have conversed, and myself have been, as a rule, baffled there, by the wind. By ten o'clock in the morning we were safely on the northern shore, and soon after two o'clock were at anchor back of Solomon's Island, in the Patuxent.*

"Drum Point Lighthouse" At Calvert Marine Museum

We had passed during the morning from one State into another. Was I mistaken in supposing that I saw greater thrift north of the Potomac? A few years ago it would have been argued that the difference was due to the greater dependence of Virginia on slave labor, that, though Maryland was still a slave State, yet it was not absolutely wedded in all its life habits to the enervating curse. This may or may not be true. I shall not attempt to decide. I cannot take leave of Virginia, where I received so much kindness, and for the character of whose citizens one must have such respect, without bringing out the early relation of the mother-country (as judged by her own writers) to the perpetuation of the system of negro slavery in the colonies.

Quoting from Doyle, I find: "In 1719 the Assembly [of South Carolina] took the further step of imposing a duty of forty pounds on all imported negroes. Had this measure been carried, it must have put an end to the slave trade so far as South Carolina was concerned. It is sad to think that such a measure was frustrated by the cupidity and jealousy of the English government. But it had become a settled maxim of colonial policy to allow the provincial assemblies no control over external trade, and in all commercial legislation to regard the profit of the English merchant rather than the social and industrial well-being of the colonists. The proprietors and the crown were for once united, and the measure was vetoed.". . . "A Virginian clergyman, writing in 1724, deplores the number of negroes, and the consequent discouragement to the poorer class of white emigrants. In South Carolina more than one attempt was made to stem the tide. In 1678, an act was passed offering a bounty on the importation of indented white servants, Irish alone excepted. That they were designed to counteract the influx of black slaves, is shown by the provision that they were to be distributed among the planters, one to every six negroes.

Patuxent may be called the dividing line between the low, sandy shore on the western side of the Chesapeake and the bolder bluffs which we find more common on the upper parts of the bay. I have never seen a more beautiful illustration of how perfectly parallel to each other, strata may be deposited, and how subsequent erosion may remove some and leave other portions, than the northern shore of the Patuxent, shows at the river's mouth and some distance inside and outside. Neither have I ever seen more tempting building-sites than these same bluffs offer. High, dry, fronting on salt water, with no fresh-water marshes near, such situations, one might infer, would be healthy. For aquatic sports the harbor of the Patuxent would afford abundant facilities. I have no doubt game is abundant both on land and on the water in season.

It is safe to say, that when the demand for country homes becomes more common among persons of culture than it now is, these bluffs will be in demand as building-sites. Of course, that will be when facilities for reaching Washington, Annapolis, and Baltimore are greatly increased."

Rothrock's vision of a future where the bluffs have been developed into country homes has largely been realized. Today, waterfront development outside of Solomon's supports a large community that has become self sustaining. This growth is largely influenced by the expansion of both Washington and Annapolis.

Aerial View Looking North from Solomon's Island

Destination: Cambridge, MD
Tuesday, July 2, 2013
(39.3 Nautical Miles, 8 Hours)

After refueling Tuesday morning in the rain, we departed Solomon's with southern winds blowing at 10 knots. Our destination was Maryland's Easter Shore. Patrick took the helm for the morning, taking a long reach across the Bay into the Choptank River. At the mouth of the river Dan took the helm for the sail up the Choptank, as the winds built to 18 knots. One hundred thirty years earlier Rothrock wrote this of his crossing, *"From the Patuxent we crossed to the Eastern Shore. Early in the morning there was a gentle breeze. It soon showed that we could not depend upon it. I therefore headed directly across to secure an anchorage where we could hold what ground we had gained, and not drift hopelessly back with the tide. It was late in the afternoon before we had any wind. A large schooner that passed across our bow, going up the bay, had drifted back several miles astern of us. Night came on, dark enough, and we were obliged to appeal to the lead-line to aid us in finding our way up the Choptank, after passing the light off Benoni's Point. We at last, fearing to venture farther, let an anchor go in Lecompte's Bay on the southern shore of the Choptank. Next morning, July 4th, we had a fair wind into Cambridge Harbor."*

As we sailed up the Choptank, *CamiCat*, still flying her asymmetrical gennaker, screamed by us as the wind built to 20 knots. She was making what looked to be 8 knots of speed to our 6 knots. Midway up the Choptank, we watched from astern as the gennaker started burying *CamiCat's* bow, causing her to snow plow water. Sliding around her stern to her starboard side, we watched as her leeward stern hull was lifting free of the water. Shortly thereafter, with a loud explosion, her gennaker blew out. With sails in shreds, *CamiCat's* crew struggling to keep the gennaker out of the water. We furled our sails, and ran up under power to assist. By the time we

117

were off her port side, Christer and John had tamed the shredded sail. Minutes later, *CamiCat* had recovered sails and both boats again were headed upriver and flying our genoas.

CamiCat Making Time on the Choptank Shortly Before Blowing Out Her Gennaker

By 3:30 in the afternoon we were approaching Hambrook Bar, looking at the outskirts of Cambridge. Along the shore is sited the Annie Oakley House, the retirement home of the famous sharpshooter and star of western shows, including Buffalo Bills Wild West Show. In 1883, at the time of Rothrock's voyage, Annie Oakley was 23 years old and just starting her career as a sharpshooter and entertainer in Cincinnati, Ohio. At the age of 57, in 1913, she and her husband Frank Butler were building their retirement home along the Choptank where they enjoyed the duck hunting and outdoors. Annie Oakley and Frank Butler lived in the house until 1917. The house is a 1 ½ story colonial-influenced bungalow that looks out across the Choptank past Hambrook Bar.

Cambridge Waterfront

A few minutes later we pulled into the Cambridge Municipal Yacht Basin and docked at the Cambridge Yacht Club (CYC). Heavy rains set in as Tim and Wendy arrived at the basin to join *CamiCat's* crew for a few days. The CYC proved a most gracious club and we spent the evening enjoying dinner in their facility as we looked out across the Choptank River.

After supper the crews set out to explore historic Cambridge. Established in 1684, Cambridge is among the oldest towns on the Bay. None of the 17th century structures remain in the city; rather it is characterized today by a collection of late 18th century to mid 20th century structures in Georgian, Queen Anne, Colonial, Greek Revival, Gothic and Romanesque Revival styles. The town is, in a word, "charming" as it melds authentic American architectural styles into a cohesive whole. Our walk, under the canopy of old growth trees, past historic homes was a trip backwards in time. One hundred thirty years ago, during Rothrock's visit, Cambridge was prosperous and growing, and many of the structures we passed date from that period of time. In 1883, Cambridge was a growing transportation center as trade, oysters, and canning fed its expansion. Today, Cambridge shows signs of the economic plight of small town

America, with many of its commercial buildings closed and shuttered. Tourism has begun to grow however, and we saw evidence of this looking upriver at the 400 room Hyatt Regency Chesapeake.

High Street in Cambridge, MD

Rothrock remained in Cambridge from July 4th through the 8th. He wrote of his visit, *"Sunday morning, July 8th, I rose early, at halfpast four. The pure glory of the morning impelled me to do so. Home-life is very apt to rob one of the cream of the day. Tired by the duties which the acquisition of daily bread imposes upon us, we shut ourselves within ourselves and brick walls. But this is not to be endured when yachting. The windows are widely open, and the earliest streak of dawn along the horizon invites you forth to receive your day's allowance of health fresh from the hand of morning. Someone says early risers are apt "to be conceited all forenoon, and stupid all afternoon." This does not apply to one in whom the aquatic life has done its full work of regeneration. Constant intercourse with nature has banished conceit, and when afternoon comes he does as most other easy-going, sensible animals do, deliberately goes to sleep and renews his stock of mental and physical vigor, that is, if at anchor. If sailing, there can be no drowsiness by day or by night, short of absolute exhaustion. I am becoming each year less surprised at how little real good the majority of our health-seekers gain by their vacation. That they reap so little benefit, is simply, as a rule, because they have not earned it, and hence do not deserve it. The professional man, if he wants the vigor of the sailor who is with him, must do as the sailor does. One new muscular fiber is added to another, when by exercise we throw off the sloth-softened old ones.*

When one can hardly keep his conscience quiet, when it reproaches him for making his vacation unduly long, then he is in a fair way to accomplish something notable on his return to duty. This sense of wasting time is often-the very best sign that vacation is doing a worthy and beneficent work. It tells how well the man has become, that he longs for activity in duty instead of longer rest.......

Christ Episcopal Church

The Choptank differs but little from the other rivers of the Chesapeake. Almost any one of them would afford a naturalist' good working-ground for an entire season. There is, however, more monotony in the country bordering the Choptank than in that along the Patuxent, for the former is nearly a dead level. Yet to me there is a quiet charm about the many-armed Choptank, which makes me wish to spend a whole vacation on its waters. During the season there is, for those who care to catch them, an abundance of fish, crabs, and oysters. And during colder months water-fowl congregate there in vast numbers.

The Choptank has for Pennsylvanians and especially for those of them in sympathy with the Society of Friends, a special historical interest. Late in December, 1682, says Bancroft, "tired of useless debates, Penn crossed the Chesapeake, to visit Friends at Choptank, and returned to his own province prepared to renew negotiation, or to submit to arbitration in England. The difficulty alluded, to grew out of settling the boundary line between Maryland and Pennsylvania. I have often been amused at a statement made by Alsop in times long antedating the American Revolution, a statement which has all the characteristic truth and point, with none of the venom (or something worse) which so often appears in the scamp's doings and sayings, "He that intends to court a Maryland girl must have something more than the tautologies of long-winded speech to carry on his designs." The brightness and unaffectedness of the modern representatives compel the belief that sham is as much despised by them as it was by their good mothers.

Cambridge may be taken as a characteristic town of the Eastern Shore. To those who have, as we had, friends there, it is always a most delightful place to visit. When we say that on the Eastern Shore one finds more traces of the old colonial life and customs than elsewhere in Maryland, no disparagement is intended. On the contrary, we may be quite sure that the social habits and the hospitality, which form such striking reminders of earlier times, are real and most sincerely genuine, and are very certain to be impressed on the memory long after more formal meetings are forgotten.

There is certainly a great future awaiting the Eastern Shore. The climate, soil, and situation all combine to make one think that its rejuvenation cannot be long delayed. During the past few years the new industry of oyster-canning has given some towns a most ' extraordinary impetus. I do not regard this, as it is now conducted, as likely to be of any great, permanent good, because it must require but a few years to remove the oysters on which present prosperity depends, unless oyster-raising becomes, as it may, a feasible thing. To this we shall allude later. But when I remember the agricultural capacity of the Eastern Shore I think its future is certain, simply because the rest of the country "hath need of it."I am convinced that in the next generation the owner of land on the Eastern Shore will be said to have, like the owner of a rich silvermine in the West, "a sure thing."

The early history of Maryland reveals some strange modes of aiding Church and State. Think of raising a church-rate by imposing a duty on tobacco! I fear many sensitive mortals in these days would wash their hands clear of the contamination caused by touch of the funds. Yet when, in 1698, the Episcopal creed was the one recognized by law, the rate was so raised. Hawks, in his "Ecclesiastical Contributions," calls to mind another striking bit of legislation: In Maryland "the vestry of Port-Tobacco Parish imposed a tax on bachelors, and the Assembly confirmed it. It, at least, indicated the sense of the Legislature that it was a luxury to have no wife, and that the privilege ought to be paid for." These are mere remembrances of the past, only alluded to because they had well-nigh been forgotten, and because they may serve to illustrate the changing phases of human thought and morals."

Destination: Trappe Creek, MD
Wednesday, July 3, 2013
(8.8 Nautical Miles, 3 Hours)

Poplar Street, Cambridge, MD

Wednesday morning had the crews of *Second Wind* and *CamiCat* enjoying "liberty" as we walked the streets of Cambridge. Individually, we set off to tour, photograph, and collect some last minute supplies in town. With southerly winds forecast at 15 knots in the afternoon, the day promised to be perfect for sailing. So, at noon we departed Cambridge with the purpose of sailing the river. Reaching down the river we headed towards Castle Haven Point on a leisurely sail. Then, turning back upriver, we headed into La Trappe Creek. Behind Martin Point, in a well protected cove, we anchored at 3:30. A short while later, *CamiCat* rafted alongside us in one of the most beautiful anchorages on the Eastern Shore. The afternoon was spent exploring the creek in our dinghy, swimming, and finally enjoying a late afternoon barbecue. After supper Christer served "dark and stormy" cocktails as we watched a beautiful sunset, followed by a night sky that was clear and filled with stars.

Aerial Photo at Anchor Behind Martin Point

Destination: Tilghman Island, MD
Thursday, July 4, 2013
(14.2 Nautical Miles, 3 Hours)

Our goal was to celebrate the Fourth of July on Tilghman Island in Napps Narrows, and we pulled anchor at 10:00 in the morning. with a planned three hour run across the Choptank River.

"Compton" Plantation House

After raising anchor, and before entering the river, we first made a quick run up La Trappe Creek to view "Compton", an 18th century plantation home located on Grubin Neck about one nautical mile from the mouth of La Trappe Creek. The plantation was once owned and improved by Samuel Stevens, 18th governor of Maryland.. Samuel Stevens inherited the plantation from his father in 1794, and would retain the property until his death in 1860. In 1822 he was elected to his first of three terms as governor. His tenure as governor saw advancement of civil liberties guaranteed in the Bill of Rights to Maryland citizens, the abolition of religious tests for state office holders, enfranchisement of the Jews, and construction of the Chesapeake and Ohio Canal. The plantation house is a relatively simple two part brick dwelling completed in two major building periods with subsequent minor alterations.

Rothrock's departure from Cambridge was to take him just outside of Napps Narrows to Poplar Island, an island that today is being reclaimed from dredged spoils. These spoils are natural materials from the bottom of the Bay, removed to deepen navigation channels and anchorages. The island is deforested and occupied by heavy construction equipment depositing the spoils across the island

Rothrock writes of his journey to Poplar Island, *"The yacht left Cambridge on the morning of July 9th, that was just before peaches were ripe. Hence we were prevented from seeing the shipment of the great peninsular crop. Peach season is, of all times, the one in which to visit the region. More information can be gained then than at any other time.*

We could notice a great change in the weather since we went down the bay a month earlier. Then the wind appeared to be continuous, or usually so, in one direction from early in the morning until towards evening. When we left Cambridge we found that the calms we had experienced off the mouth of the Potomac and in crossing from the Patuxent to the Eastern Shore were but the first of a series. From Cambridge up, we were reasonably sure of a morning breeze (though often a very gentle one), then a noon-day calm, then more or less threatening weather towards evening. Not that evening always brought its squall, for it did not, but that it nearly always attempted to, if such an expression be allowable.

Looking West from Napps Narrows

Starting from Cambridge at 9 A.M. with a fair breeze, which died out, it was full twelve hours before we dropped our anchor in the snug little harbor between Poplar Island and the main-land. I was particularly anxious for a good, rousing wind that day, as my friend, Captain Thomas Howard, was with me, and I wanted to show my little sloop to the best advantage. When we stopped for the night it was blowing hard from the south. The last two or three miles of our run were made before a wind under which the yacht fairly staggered; and as we passed over the shoal water in the darkness, before reaching our anchorage, I knew that if we made any mistake and ran aground, the mast would go like a reed in a hurricane. In spite of the wind, which whistled vigorously through the rigging, we lay down in a most comfortable frame of mind. We could feel the boat tugging away at the anchor, but having full confidence in the strength of our cable and in the holding power of the anchor, we could sleep undisturbed."

Working Boats on Tilghman Island

Our winds for the day were more reliable as we again enjoyed southerly winds at about 15 knots, and our sail into Napps Narrows was quick and uneventful. At 1:00 in the afternoon, fighting a strong current through the Narrows, we pulled into Napps Narrows Marina for the holiday. There we made the last of our crew changes as Eric and Shanna joined *CamiCat's* crew and Tim and Wendy departed. Following lunch at the marina restaurant the crew dispersed, with one group borrowing the marina's courtesy bicycles to ride the length of Tilghman Island, and another group headed to the pool.

Tilghman Island derives its name from the Tilghman family who owned the island for almost a century starting in 1752. In 1840 James Seth purchased the island from General Tilghman and developed the island by selling off parcels of land to farmers and oystermen. When oyster dredging was legalized in Maryland, the watermen of Tilghman joined the boat building industry and development expanded. By 1890 steamboat service was established to the island, and seafood processing expanded.

Aerial Photo of Napps Narrows

Although the oyster and seafood industry on the Bay is dying, the island has become a tourist destination as Washington and Baltimore residents escape to the Eastern Shore for holidays and weekends. The growth of Bread & Breakfasts, restaurants, upscale weekend homes, and fishing boats all enhance the tourist industry. But, it is the simple lifestyle on the island that draws weekenders away from the complexity of city living.

Aerial Photo Looking West from Napps Narrows

Destination: Queenstown, MD
Friday, July 5, 2013
(13.9 Nautical Miles, 3 Hours 20 Minutes)

Friday morning gave Christer an opportunity to fly his drone for the first time from solid ground. The large gravel lot behind Napps Narrows Marina provided the perfect opportunity to replace pontoons for wheels and complete more aerial photography. After two successful flights, breakfast was served, and the boats were made ready for the day's sail.

Running Up Eastern Bay

We departed mid morning and made our way back into the Chesapeake heading north to Queenstown. Sailing inside Poplar Island, we turned up into Eastern Bay and headed around Parsons Island into Prospect Bay, and finally into the Kent Narrows.

Rothrock traveled to Queenstown by way of Annapolis and wrote of his voyage, *"Leaving Poplar Island next morning, we threaded our way out into the bay past the southern end of Kent Island. It should here be stated that a light-house has been erected within a few years on the end of the bar which "makes out" from the southern point of Kent. Outside of that bar is one of the deepest parts of the bay. My chart shows, for a single point there, eighteen fathoms.*

Bridge Closing In Kent Narrows

Kent Narrows separates Kent Island from the Delmarva Peninsula on its eastern side. It provides a shortened route past Kent Island into the Chester River. Instead of revisiting Annapolis as Rothrock had, we sailed directly to Queenstown. Strong currents, shallow water, and a draw bridge that operates on a restricted schedule combine to make the Kent Narrows waterway more treacherous than an open water route. And with a strong current carrying us into the narrows, the journey past the draw bridge provided more excitement than might be hoped for.

Once past the Narrows, we motored into the Chester River

through a narrow dredged channel with Kent Island to our port side. Kent Island is the largest island in the Chesapeake Bay. The first English settlement on the island, Kent Fort, was founded in 1631. This marks Kent Island as the oldest English settlement within the state of Maryland, and the third oldest permanent English settlement in the United States. Until the 19th century, Kent Island supported the farming of tobacco and corn. But, by 1850 the town of Stevensville had become a steamboat landing, and railroads that extended to the Stevensville Rail Station opened the town as a transportation hub. One hundred years later, the island would dramatically open itself to expanded development with the completion of the Chesapeake Bay Bridge. The bridge opened the island to western shore traffic, and development quickly overran the island. Today, residential neighborhoods and commercial strips dominate the island.

Rothrock wrote of Kent Island, *"The low shores of Kent Island, in spite of their monotony, were very attractive. Besides this, too, the island played a very important part in the early history of the country, being claimed both by Virginia and by Maryland.*

In 1631 the Virginia Assembly sent a surveyor named William Clayborne to take possession of the island. It was claimed both "by royal grant and by actual purchase from the Indians." It appears to have been occupied several years earlier by settlers and by Indian traders from Virginia. Besides its fertility, its position from an offensive or defensive point of view, as well as its value as a trading-post, made both colonies eager to possess it. Clayborne was a resolute, and probably a somewhat reckless, man, belonging to a class still largely represented in our frontier States. Things remained in an unsettled and somewhat threatening condition on the island until the spring of 1635, when Clayborne took steps which inaugurated open hostilities. In the naval skirmish which ensued, three Virginians and one Marylander were killed. Clayborne, being worsted, was obliged to leave the island. Maryland now took possession, and Captain Evelyn was made its governor. The inhabitants being mainly from Virginia were naturally enough hostile to Maryland, and the new governor appears to have had anything but an amicable community to deal with. Accordingly, we find it was not long before he proclaimed martial law. For a time, at least, there seems to have been no bloodshed, though it was necessary to refer the case to the home authorities in England. By them, after much debate, it was finally assigned to Maryland. In 1641, authority was given by Maryland to the Kent Islanders to wage war against the neighboring "Susquehannock" Indians, who had become exceedingly troublesome. At first, the relations between them and the islanders appear to have been of the most friendly character, but only for a time; it was nothing but the inevitable conflict between a higher and an inferior race when brought into actual contact. One or the other must ultimately give way. About 1644 Clayborne renewed his attempt on Kent Island, and, after holding possession for a year or two, was finally ejected by Calvert, of Maryland, who himself died very shortly afterwards; and his death, as Bancroft tells us, "foreboded for the colony new disasters."

Bowlingly Plantation House

Continuing our journey, we sailed up the Chester with southwesterly winds. We set a course for Queenstown, the original seat of Queen Anne's County. As we approached the channel into Queenstown Creek, we discovered that our starboard engine would not start. After a few minutes of "fidgeting," we finally came into harbor under one engine. Directly in line with the channel into the creek is sited the Bowlingly plantation home. Built in 1733, Bowlingly overlooks the channel into Queenstown Creek and across the Chester River. It is among the earliest dated structures in the central Eastern Shore, and its scale and size are indicative of the significance of the house at the time of its construction. Bowlingly, according to the contemporary account of a local militia officer Major Thomas Emory, was pillaged by the British during the War of 1812. At dawn on August 13, 1813, a flotilla of English ships landed at Bowlingly's wharf. The British troops severely damaged the house before encountering the local militia. Other accounts maintain that the British landed across the creek from Bowlingly at Blakeford. The local militia, separated from the numerically superior British force by Queenstown Creek, had enough time to retreat toward Centreville. The house has been renovated several times, and today includes features associated with at least five different periods of construction.

Queenstown Creek

Once inside the harbor we again rafted up with *CamiCat* for our last night together. The evening we shared turned to celebration, as the cooks baked brownies in observance of Shana's Birthday. With toasts all around, it was a bittersweet evening knowing the three week voyage was at an end.

Destination: Magothy River, MD
Saturday, July 6, 2013
(13.9 Nautical Miles, 3 Hours 20 Minutes)

At sunrise on Saturday we cast off from *CamiCat*, raised our anchor, and headed out of Queenstown Harbor. Winds were still from the southwest and we were soon headed down the Chester River. Making 5 ½ knots, we were headed for home on the Magothy. Rothrock's experience coming out of the Chester on July 12, 1883, was captured in these words, *"Sometimes for weeks the yachtsman has to do almost constantly with calm or squall, and the alternatives narrow down to drifting or scudding. We apparently had entered upon one of those trying periods. As we came out of Chester River, there was a bare suspicion of wind. No one could say where it came from, first south, then west, then nowhere. After exercise of great patience and muscle we had worked, by three P.M., out into the bay again. Meanwhile, the clouds were piling up dark and threatening, and the falling barometer told that beyond doubt a storm was impending. Together with these, there were obvious warnings there was a peculiar, hazy atmosphere and an absolute stillness which led us to think that when it did come, it would be severe. The cloud-bank moved, from the southeast, west, then toward the north, gathering, as it went, into a heavy, blue-gray or lead-colored (but not black) mass. There is something in waiting for such an onset not unlike the feeling with which the soldier waits for an enemy's charge. It was certain to come, and it was certain to be full of danger. Those who- can best control their feelings are the most fortunate. The man who under such circumstances boasts that he has no fear is not so much to be envied for his supposed fortitude as pitied for his lack of truthfulness."*

Baltimore Light

We were more fortunate in our endeavors, and in spite of softening breezes maintained 5 knots of speed using one engine and with our genoa and main sails set. By 9 a.m. we were off Love Point and headed west towards the Baltimore Light, located just outside the mouth of the Magothy River. Baltimore Light is a privately-owned caisson lighthouse that was first lit in 1908, twenty five years after Rothrock's cruise. It marks the channel which leads northwest to the opening of the Patapsco River, which then leads into the Baltimore harbor. At the time of its construction, it was the world's tallest caisson lighthouse. In June 2006, Baltimore Light was sold at auction to private owners by the General Services Administration for

$260,000. The U.S. Coast Guard still maintains the right to operate a light on the structure. Although a lighthouse had been requested at the site since 1890, it was not until 1904 that construction actually began. In October of that year a violent storm struck the construction site, upturning the caisson, and sending it to the bottom of the Bay. The contractor defaulted on the work, and it was not until late in 1905 that construction could resume. The lens was finally installed and the light lit in 1908. It was among the last of the lighthouses to be constructed on the Chesapeake. In 1964 the Baltimore Light became the first and only American lighthouse powered by nuclear energy. Two years later the reactor was removed and a conventional electric generator was installed. Currently the lighthouse is solar-powered.

As Rothrock approached this same location 130 years earlier he was set upon by a fierce summer storm. He writes, *There was a large schooner which came out of the river with us. She had headed northward for Baltimore, and we were endeavoring to enter Magothy River, to the west. First we saw the schooner take down her topsail, then her foresail, then her jib, and then her mainsail. We knew that there was no time to waste. It was evident that the captain, looking to the windward, had reason for his prompt action. So we lowered our jib and put a double reef in our mainsail. We hoped to carry enough of canvas to run into Magothy River. The bay was still as calm as a mill-pond after we had shortened sail. But in a few minutes, darkness suddenly shut the schooner to the north of us out from view. In an instant later the rush of the wind was upon us. The stanch little boat endured the tremendous strain so bravely that we were at once reassured as to her seaworthiness; and she held her way toward the harbor. "Mose" braced himself against the tiller, and, though a powerful man, it required all his strength to keep the boat from luffing, as her jib was down. In less than five minutes the waves were breaking over us, and the spray dashed into our faces until we were no longer able to endure it. If we could have stood at our posts the boat would have gone safely into the Magothy River. But we could not, and there was nothing left for us to do, except to lower the mainsail and go to the southward, under bare poles, before the wind. This had become the more necessary as we were now among larger vessels, all of which were scudding. Hence, if for no other reason than to keep out of their way, we were obliged to do likewise.*

The intensity of the wind did not last more than twenty minutes; but while it did last our speed was fearful. To make matters worse, we were towing the yawl-boat, which ran up on to us and would drive its iron-clad bow into the stern of the yacht with tremendous force. As the darkness "lifted," we saw coming down astern of us a large schooner. To keep out of its way, the jib was hoisted. It was impossible to prevent the yacht from "yawing" when she rose on the waves, and then the jib would fly from side to side until each time the sheet tightened it made our heavy bowsprit quiver like a reed. Soon after, we hoisted the peak of the mainsail. We soon saw that there was no danger now so long as we kept going before the wind, for, in spite of the high seas which followed us, not a drop of water came on board after we headed south. The buoyancy of the boat was wonderful. And, from that day forth, I felt that my yacht more than compensated for being slower than some others, by being safer. The iron ballast, low down and well fastened, evidently, was just where it was doing the most good."

Rothrock would be driven down the Bay and into Annapolis for the night before returning back into the Magothy a day later. He writes of his return to the Magothy *"The day after the squall we started again to go up the bay. Leaving Annapolis early in the morning, the breeze, though ahead, was promising enough, so far as its strength was concerned, but on our very first tack it died away entirely, and we drifted hopelessly. About two o'clock it revived just a little, and we headed for Magothy River. By dint of hard rowing, we at last rounded Sandy Point, and then reached the mouth of the river. Then turning south into Deep Creek we anchored for the night. For small craft, a more desirable haven than this could not well be found. Later in the evening I discovered that the water was as well stocked with pickerel as the shore was with wood-ticks. The channel had from six to eight feet of water in it, but along-shore it was shallow and muddy. In the shoal water the interesting water-weed"* (Anacharis *Canadensis) was growing in the greatest profusion, and as we rowed through the tangled mass the startled pickerel could be seen darting on all sides of us. The plant was in full bloom."*

Gibson Island Shoreline

Fortunately, We were not forced by storm from entering the Magothy, so we steered a course towards the narrow mouth of the River. To starboard of the channel into the river is the private community of Gibson Island. This community was developed in 1922, almost forty years after Rothrock's cruise. The community was designed by the Olmstead Brothers of Brookline, Massachusetts, who at that time were the most prominent landscape architectural design firm in the nation. Developed as a private summer resort on the Bay, it was intended that "attractive persons of moderate means" would summer over to enjoy days of leisure. The development includes a golf course, sailing club, tennis, and swimming. During the 1920's Gibson Island was marketed as the "Newport of the South" and attracted members including socialites, businessmen, and politicos from Baltimore. Originally designed to include 423 residential properties and two 18 hole golf courses, final development included only 190 residences and a 9 hole golf course. Sailing past the island, we viewed an eclectic collection of homes of various styles and materials dotting the shoreline.

We passed Deep Creek to our portside as we headed upriver. These waters would be unrecognizable to Rothrock today. Gone are the sea grasses and pickerel. The entire environment that Rothrock spoke of in such detail in his book has been destroyed and replaced by residential shoreline development, with piers, marinas, and boats lining the entire waterway.

Rothrock wrote of the Magothy *"The chief productions of the region appeared to be melons, peaches, and "garden truck." Proximity to Baltimore doubtless made such interests very lucrative there. The busy freighting-season for these productions was just coming on, and it was with difficulty that I convinced one farmer that I could not be induced to do his carrying for him."* Now, houses along the shoreline replace the farms that once supplied Baltimore with fruits and vegetables. Agriculture has disappeared as an industry on the Magothy, and in its place shoreline residential communities support commuters working in Annapolis, Baltimore, and Washington.

Three and a half nautical miles upriver from Deep Creek, we pulled up to our dock. It was almost three weeks to the hour from the time we cast off to begin our voyage until we returned to our pier. My day, however, was not over. After packing an overnight bag, Cece and I were soon on a train headed north with the intention of meeting our granddaughter for the first time.

Endings never really come to pass, good or bad. Rather, life overlaps and blurs with one story transforming into a new story. Rothrock's story of a vacation cruise on the Bay 130 years earlier had given way to our story of the Chesapeake. And on this day, that story was giving way to a new story with a new life. Our story is a part of a collective story, with no telling where it may lead.

But one hope that we all shared was that future stories would include a healthier outlook for the Bay. The Chesapeake is a remarkable treasure whose survival is now clearly threatened by man and his development.   Much has changed on the Bay since Rothrock's voyage. The profusion of sea grasses are gone from the Bay, and with them the pickerel. The abundance of oysters, fish, and crab has all retreated behind overfishing, pollution, and overdevelopment along the shoreline. The bald eagle, bottlenose porpoises, rock fish, and frogs are all in retreat.   In the 1970s, the Chesapeake Bay was found to contain one of the planet's first identified marine dead zones, where waters were so depleted of oxygen that they were unable to support life, resulting in massive fish kills. Today the Bay's dead zones are estimated to kill 75,000 tons of bottom-dwelling clams and worms each year, weakening the base of the estuary's food chain and robbing the blue crab in particular of a primary food source.   More responsible stewardship is desperately needed.

CHAPTER IV
WHO SHOULD GO CRUISING

Rothrock writes, *"Who should go cruising? There is a constantly-increasing number of young and middle-aged men who, under the exactions of daily duty, find themselves each spring physically below par. Many of them cannot afford the cost of a prolonged trip by the ordinary means of travel, even if it be undertaken in the interest of health. Indeed, it is by no means certain that such a vacation would yield the largest return, for the simple reason that there is nothing for the individual to do, save to pay his bills and be taken care of. Thus the stimulus of personal activity and of responsibility is missed, and with it, also, that complete change in mental occupation which a cruise is sure to afford, if it be such as I have tried to describe."*

"A Snapshot of Recreational Boating in America" by Dr. Glenn E. Haas, Professor Emeritus, Colorado State University in 2010 reported that 82 million adult Americans participated in recreational boating in 2009. 12.7 million boats were registered in the United States that year, and over 30.8 billion dollars was spent on recreational boating sales and services.

If yachting and recreational boating were in their infancy in 1883, by 2013 it has become very big business as more and more Americans have found the waterways their recreational outlet. By

2020 projections call for 60.4 million motor boaters; 23.3 million canoers; 21.1 million personal water craft users; 20.9 million rafters; 19.1 million water-skiers; 13.5 million kayakers; 11.4 million sailors; and 9.7 million rowers competing for use of America's waterways.

Since the Industrial Revolution, America has become a nation obsessed by its health and diet. Physical fitness and healthy exercise have emerged as an American preoccupation. Health clubs, gyms, bike clubs, yoga, sports fields, weight rooms, golf courses, racket clubs, and pools adorn our land. Boating and sailing, like so many other endeavors, has emerged as a healthy lifestyle choice in our collective American obsession to stop the aging process.

Rothrock writes, *"The essential substratum upon which health must rest is muscular exertion. Muscular fiber comes only when earned. However valuable as aids, I doubt whether all the tonics of the shops, alone, ever created an ounce of muscle. Cruising affords not only the incentive to, but the opportunity for, healthful exercise.*

The trips I have described were made in a small vessel (six tons). A party of, say, four congenial companions could make such, or more distant ones, in a larger boat, spending a month in doing so, and, after paying for other vessel, hiring a captain and a cook, purchasing the provisions, still find that the expense for each man did not exceed fifty dollars for the whole trip. They could do this, I have said, if they were congenial companions. If they were not, the first week would probably end the cruise. Is there any other way ' in which so much health and pleasure could be had for so small a sum?"

Inflation drove the cost of our cruise well beyond the average cost of fifty dollars per person that Rothrock was able to budget for in 1883. In the case of the *Second Wind*, costs included fuel, marinas, food, boat insurance, dockage, and boat carrying costs. Typical monthly carrying costs are budgeted at $825. The cost for a three week cruise included $425 for 107 gallons of diesel fuel; $862 for transient slip fees and moorings; $239 for repairs and marine supplies; and $285 for the captain and skipper's restaurant dining.

Provisioning costs ran about $400 including food and drink. Total cost per person ran $600, a twelvefold increase in cost since 1883.

Rothock wrote, *"Probably this never would have been written but from the fact that no one here has yet tried to write up a cruise as the author of "Rob Roy on the Jordan" has done for England. That it was needed in that water-loving land, and that it was acceptable, is shown from the fact that the book speedily passed through several editions. No such success is anticipated for this effort. It will have accomplished its work if it stimulates someone else to do better."*

A search for "Sailing Books" on the Amazon web site returned 16,399 book titles. 316 of these books are listed as published within the last 90 days. With the explosion of recreational boating, there has also occurred a comparable explosion in the number and variety of books written about the boating experience. An almost mystical encounter is bound to touch the soul of any sailor at some point in his journey. Whether at sunset or sunrise as they gaze across an anchorage, at mid-day watching a powerful storm move across the open water, sitting in a quiet cove watching the herons fish along the shoreline, or at midnight with a sky filled with stars in greater numbers and brilliance than can be reasonably comprehended, a sailor invariably experiences the world in a unique and special way. The thin veil between heaven and earth often disappears on the water, and Rothrock's book, like so many afterwards, touches on the healing power of communing with nature and the sea.

Rothrock wrote his book inspired by *"The Rob Roy on the Jordan: A Canoe Cruise in Palestine and Egypt"* written by John Macgregor in 1869. Macgregor was introduced to canoeing during a visit to the United States in 1858 and turned to boating when a railroad accident left him severely injured. He designed a 15 foot long 'double-ended' canoe modeled after the Indian canoes of North America, to be used with a double-bladed paddle. He named the boat Rob Roy after the celebrated Scottish outlaw of the same name, to whom he was related. During the 1860s, he had similar boats built and he sailed and paddled them in Europe, the Baltic and the Middle East. An adventurer, Macgregor became internationally famous as an author and lecturer.

"Who should not go cruising? First, those who expect nothing but comfort, and who cannot endure plain living, or those to whom monotonous drifting one day, with possibly a tempest tossing the next, is a greater annoyance than a week of pleasant sailing and free, open-air life can compensate for. Second, those whose education has been so neglected that they have never been taught to enjoy exposure for the manhood which it brings. This feeling is to some a natural gift, or, if you prefer, an unconquerable longing; to others it must be an acquisition. Physicians know that a very great trouble they have in dealing with ailing ones is, that to order them to a camp or to a cruise, would be to make life so intolerable that no good could come of it. Hence, then, in the interest of health, it is part of a liberal education to love the winds and the waves, as well as the mountain-glens. The most profound thinker of this age says, when in one of his lighter moods, "Exclusive devotion to work has the result that amusements cease to please; and, when relaxation becomes imperative, life becomes dreary from lack of its sole interest, the interest in business. Life is not for learning, nor is life for working, but learning and working are for life." An early and a retained fondness for yachting and for angling has prolonged, no one knows how many years, Herbert Spencer's active, useful career.

There is a third class who should not go cruising. I mean such as enjoy being weak, those creatures to whom bronzed skins and excessive vitality are an abomination. To such we would say, Stay at home, by all means! In the whole world out of doors there is no place for you.

"Still breathe we this high air with rapture, still
See earth dilated to a palace large,
Roofed with blue bravery of the cloud-sailed sky."

A fourth class should be named as unfit for cruising, those who are confirmed invalids, who have passed the point at which they can make strength faster than such a vacation, or such an occupation, would use it. To advise these to leave comfortable homes is a moral wrong which admits of no justification.

Within a few years "the canoe" has awakened a profound interest in the United States. The constantly-increasing number of those who yield each summer to the fascination of the paddle shows that there must be, as we know there is, infinite pleasure in skimming our inland waters. Nothing that has been written in advocacy of yachting is to be construed as against "canoeing." They belong together as forms of the same recreation, each having its sphere, and each yielding a full return for the time and money expended, providing discretion rules the individual."

CHAPTER V
BEYOND THE CHESAPEAKE

Rothrock's voyages and his book did not stop on the Magothy River as our voyage did. His voyage extended on to the head of the Chesapeake, through the Chesapeake and Delaware Canal, and on into the Delaware Bay where he cruised until July 21st, 1883. He returned to Camden, NJ, with the *Martha*, and one month later on August 27, 1883, again departed Camden, NJ, to return *Martha* to the Chesapeake and her winter quarters in Cambridge, Maryland.

He writes, *"Nothing more clearly indicates the unsettled character of the human mind than that we tire of our pleasures. Nothing shows more strongly the discipline of life than the patience with which well-ordered minds toil on, until the hour comes when they may fairly enjoy the freedom of doing as they will. I had waited and worked for my vacation. I enjoyed the pleasure it brought until, sated, I longed again for work.*

Salt air and water, physical labor and mental rest, had done much towards renewing my youth, and promised to do more. Even a yachtsman may realize that life has duties more important than cruising. Autumn was approaching, as the russet blades of corn plainly indicated. This meant work."

Rothrock went on in his career and work to become known as "the father of Pennsylvania forestry" and to distinguish himself for his contributions to North American botany. He championed environmental causes, advocating for a Pennsylvania reforestation program. He endeavored to rally public opinion, obtain the cooperation of Pennsylvania's political leadership, and develop effective government-private sector collaboration in establishing and administering a reforestation program in a state that previously had no public wilderness or forest preserves.

Rothrock's work also included advancing forestry education and the development of state parks. His work in Pennsylvania led the way to the development of similar programs in other states. His scientific studies were at the forefront of a major transition in botany from a largely "taxonomic activity" to "plant physiology and pathology".

He finishes his book, "*This ended the cruising of the "Martha" for the season. The staunch little sloop, now laid up for the winter in Cambridge harbor, awaits new duties in the coming season, 1884.*

Who that reads Tam o' Shanter can fail to see an overflowing genius in every line? Burns must have been placed among the poets, though he had written nothing save,

> "*But pleasures are like poppies spread,*
> *You seize the flow'r, its bloom is shed;*
> *Or like the snow falls in the river,*
> *A moment white, then melts forever;*
> *Or like the borealis race,*
> *That flit ere you can point their place;*
> *Or like the rainbow's lovely form*
> *Evanishing amid the storm.*"

Though every idea there is a genuine reflection from nature which inspired the poet, still, when I look back over my three months of quiet cruising, those glowing lines do not express the facts to me. True, the pleasures departed with the days, but the memory of them remains as part of me; and is as truly a mental treasure to me, as if derived from the pages of any

151

author.

Far more real and full is the stately verse of Tennyson,

> *"But in my spirit will I dwell,*
> *And dream my dream, and hold it true;*
> *For tho' my lips may breath Adieu!'*
> *I cannot think the thing farewell!"*

THE END